# MOVING GRAPHICS

New directions in motion design
Les nouvelles tendances du motion design
Nuevas tendencias en animación gráfica
Nuove direzioni nel design in movimento

promopress

Motion Design is a branch of graphic design in that it uses graphic design principles in a film or video context (or other temporally evolving visual medium) through the use of animation or filmic techniques. With the dramatic growth of digital media in recent years, more and more designers from all over the world have been involved in this area. This book with an interactive DVD package presents the latest works from the world's leading motion graphic studios. The striking works submitted by 79 talented international studios are categorised according to the following genres: "Art & Culture", "Commercial Advertising", "Show Opener" and "Fun & Others". The accompanying DVD contains all the featured works, which allows the readers to watch the motion designs repeatedly and research the details in the works. The collected outstanding works are not to be missed!

Le Motion Design est une branche du design graphique ayant recours aux principes de conception graphique dans le contexte d'un film ou d'une vidéo (ou de tout autre ressource visuelle en mouvement) à travers des animations ou techniques cinématographiques. Le développement spectaculaire des médias numériques ces dernières années, a de plus en plus poussé les designers du monde entier à s'investir dans ce domaine. Ce livre et son coffret DVD interactif présentent les dernières œuvres des principaux studios mondiaux de graphisme animé. Ces œuvres marquantes de 79 studios internationaux talentueux sont classées selon les catégories suivantes : « art et culture », « publicité commerciale », « ouverture de galas » et « variétés & autres». Le DVD joint contient toutes les œuvres présentées et permet aux lecteurs de visionner à souhait les conceptions animées mais également de faire des recherches sur leur contenu. Une collection d'ouvrages exceptionnels à ne pas manquer !

El *motion design* es una rama del diseño gráfico por cuanto explota los principios de esta disciplina en película o en video (u otros medios visuales de desarrollo temporal) mediante el empleo de la animación o de otras técnicas fílmicas. En años recientes, con el espectacular crecimiento de los medios digitales, un número cada vez mayor de diseñadores del mundo entero se ha ido sumando a esta práctica. El libro que presentamos, con su complemento interactivo en DVD, ofrece las obras más innovadoras de estudios punteros de todo el mundo en el ámbito del *motion design*. Los llamativos trabajos presentados por 79 excelentes estudios internacionales aparecen clasificados por géneros: "Arte y cultura", "Publicidad comercial", "Presentaciones", "Ocio y demás". El DVD adicional exhibe todas las obras presentadas, lo que permite a los lectores contemplar repetidamente estos diseños animados y examinarlos en detalle. ¡Un festival de obras sobresalientes!

Il *motion design* è un ramo del graphic design nel quale si sfruttano principi di *graphic design* nel contesto di un film o di un video (o di qualsiasi altro mezzo visuale che evolva nel tempo) mediante tecniche filmiche o di animazione. Con l'impressionante crescita dei mezzi digitali negli ultimi anni, questa area sta richiamando un numero sempre crescente di designer da tutto il mondo. Con l'ausilio di un pacchetto DVD interattivo, questo libro presenta le ultime opere dei più importanti studi di *motion graphic* al mondo. Le spettacolari opere presentate da 79 studi tra i più ricchi di talento sulla scena internazionale sono suddivise in base al genere: "Arte e cultura", "Propaganda commerciale", "Apertura dello spettacolo", "Varie e divertenti". Il DVD allegato contiene tutte le opere descritte e permetterà al lettore di ammirare più volte questi esempi di design in movimento e di esaminare i lavori in dettaglio. Una collezione di opere eccezionali da non perdere!

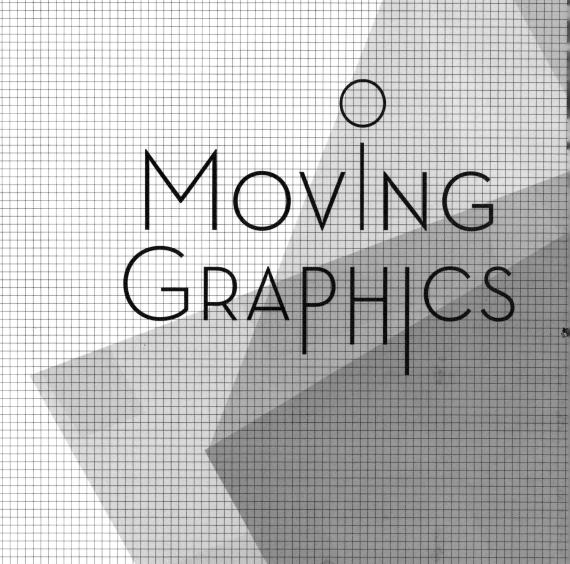

# Moving Graphics

# CONTENTS

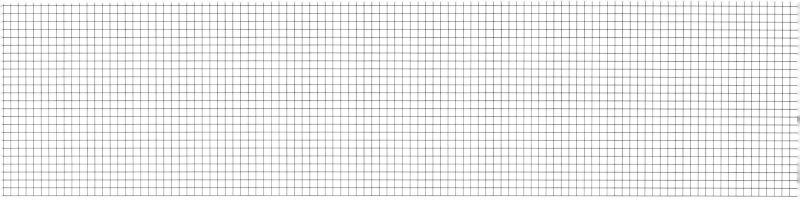

## SHOW OPENER

## FUN & OTHERS

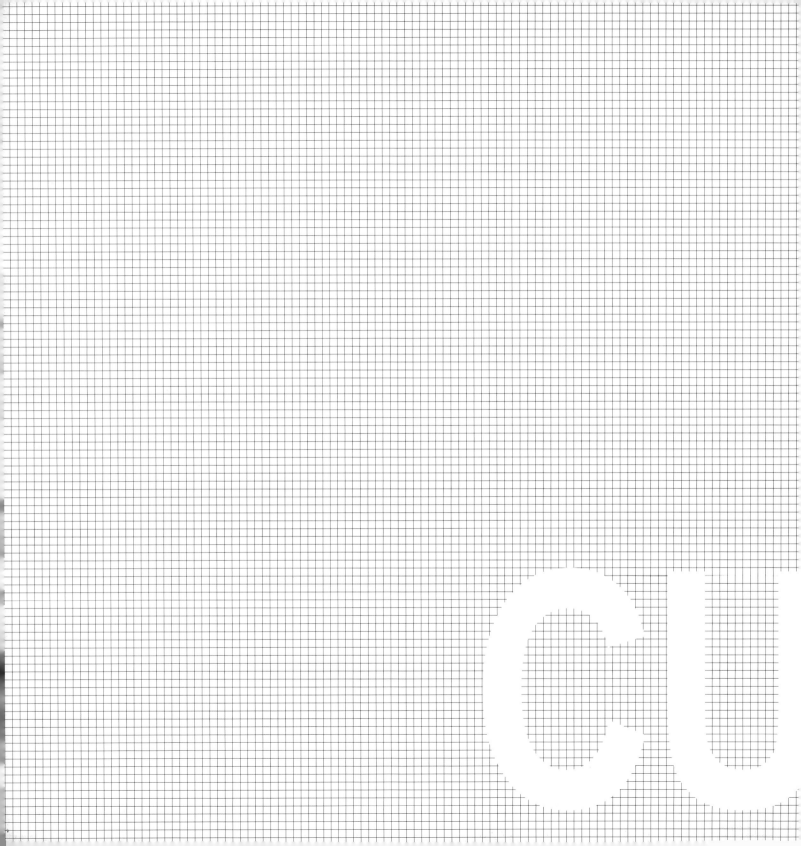

## Project: Cutting

**Designer:** Yan-Ting Chen;
**Client:** Musicut;
**Software:** After Effect, Premiere, 3ds Max, Bonjou, Photoshop.

As a traditional Chinese art, paper-cutting was very popular in the past. In this short film, the "cutting-magician" uses her paper-cutting to embellish the whole city. The streets are connected with red paper and the buildings are covered by paper. The growing red pattern represents a new vitality of paper-cutting art.

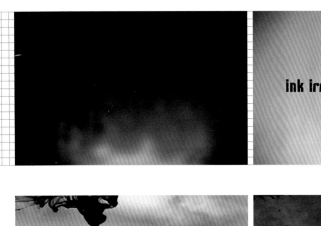
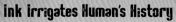

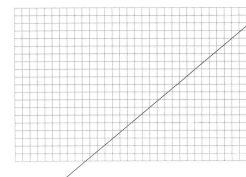

**Project:** The Word

**Designer:** Yan-Ting Chen.
**Client:** Self-promotion.
**Software:** After Effect, Premiere, 3ds Max, Bonjou, Photoshop.

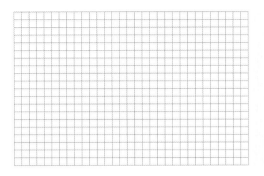

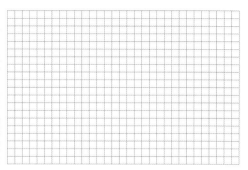

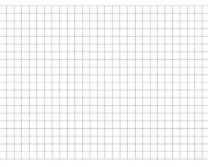

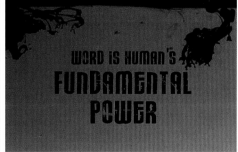

This project designed by Yan-Ting Chen tries to adopt ancient ink to reflect a sense of history. And also it adopts the images of letters to express the meaning of the work – "Language is built up by words, and writing records time of human being. Thus, word is our fundamental power."

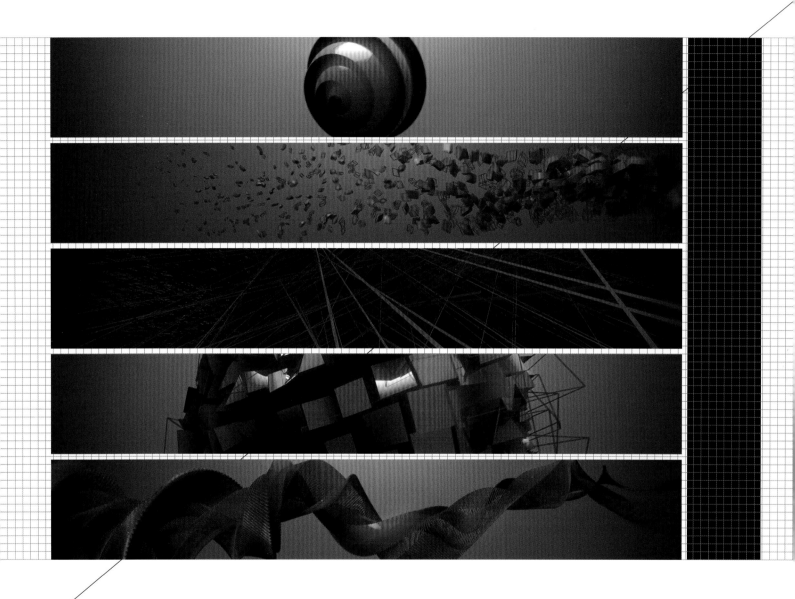

**Project:** Flux

**Designer:** Candaş Şişman;
**Client:** Plato Art Space;
**Software:** After Effects & Cinema 4D.

The video installation Flux is designed by young artist Candaş Şişman. It can be defined as a digital animation which is inspired from the structural features of some of Ilhan Koman's works like Pi, 3D Moebius, Whirlpool and To Infinity. The red circle, which is colored in reference to the red radiators of Ogre, is traced in a morphological transformation which re-interprets the formal approach of Koman's works. The continuous movement sometimes connotes the formal characteristics of Pi, 3D Moebius, Whirlpool and To Infinity, as well as the original formal interpretations of the design principles of the works. In Flux, Koman's design process in the making of the Pi series has been treated as the emerging of a sphere from a two-dimensional circle by the principle of increasing the surface, and that simple direction is re-interpreted in a digital medium.

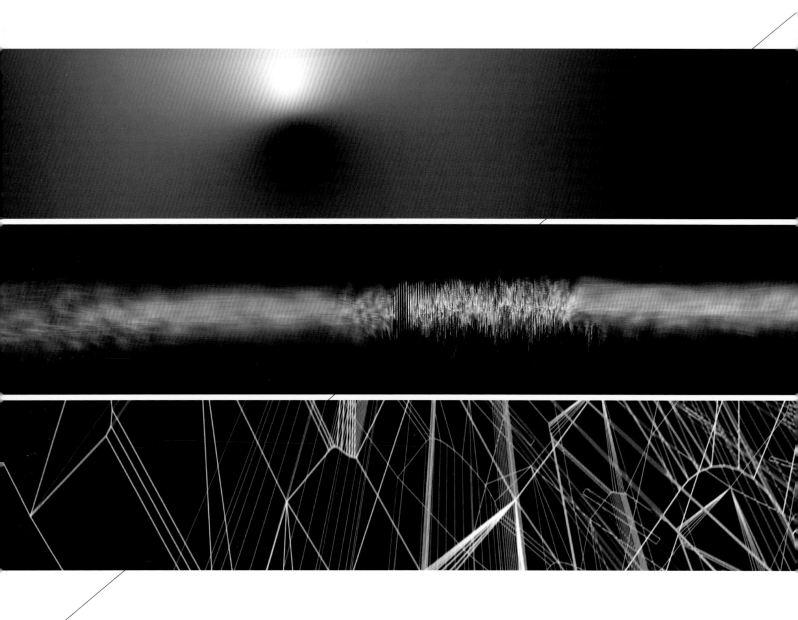

**Project: KNİTT**

Designer: Candaş Şişman;
Client: Istanbul 2010 European Capital of Culture;
Software: After Effects & Cinema 4D.

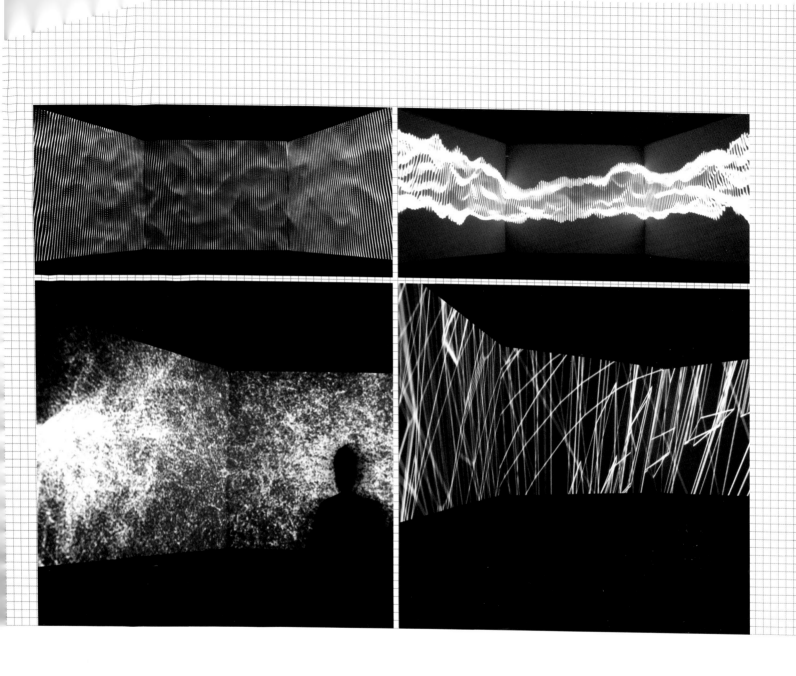

This work is an audiovisual installation on the surrounded screen with surround sound. The designer just wants to take audiences to experience "surroundings", "balance", "virtual" and "reality" in the work with an amazing combined effect of sound and visuals. The work also gives a feel that everything is affecting us and our environments.

**Project:** Polygon | Stdm and Polygon | Spring Circus

**Designer:** Serge Tardif;
**Client:** Self-promotion;
**Software:** Cinema 4D & After Effects.

This is a self-promotional work designed by Serge Tardif. The aim is to integrate the abstract elements and simple polygons in the figurative environment, and make a balance between the references and abstract images, then make the viewers understand the meaning of the work. He works with the textures and lights to express the metaphor and spirit, adopting Cinema 4D and After Effects.

**Project:** Triangle

**Design Firm:** Onur Senturk TV;
**Designer:** Onur Senturk;
**Client:** V group, 00;
**Software:** After Effects & 3ds Max.

Triangle is a video work created for the book "*Black Material*" which showcases Robert Knoke's artworks. The designer wants to create tense harmony between geometrical forms and organic movements in the work. Combustion helps him to expand the application of "black material" with his strong music and sound design.

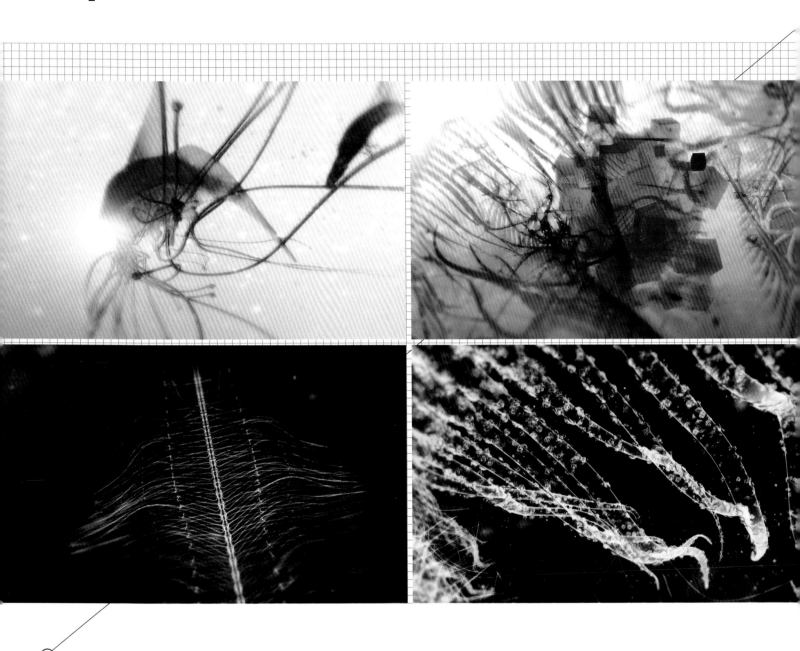

# Project: Pororoca

**Design Firm:** Neither-Field;
**Designer:** Scott Pagano;
**Client:** Laura Escude;
**Software:** Houdini, Maya, After Effects.

This is an exploration in mysterious underwater world which is inspired by the forms and movement of sea life and the microorganisms. The hybrid organic and synthetic creatures wander through the heavy waters in concert with the cinematic soundtrack.

**Project:** Bipolar

**Design Firm:** MateriaBlanca – Estudio Visual;
**Designer:** Jeison Barba;
**Software:** After Effects & Cinema 4D.

This short promo is an experimental animation designed by Jeison Barba. Lights and geometric shapes gradually appear and blend harmoniously in the middle of an abstract environment for which the designer tries to create a perfect visual effect.

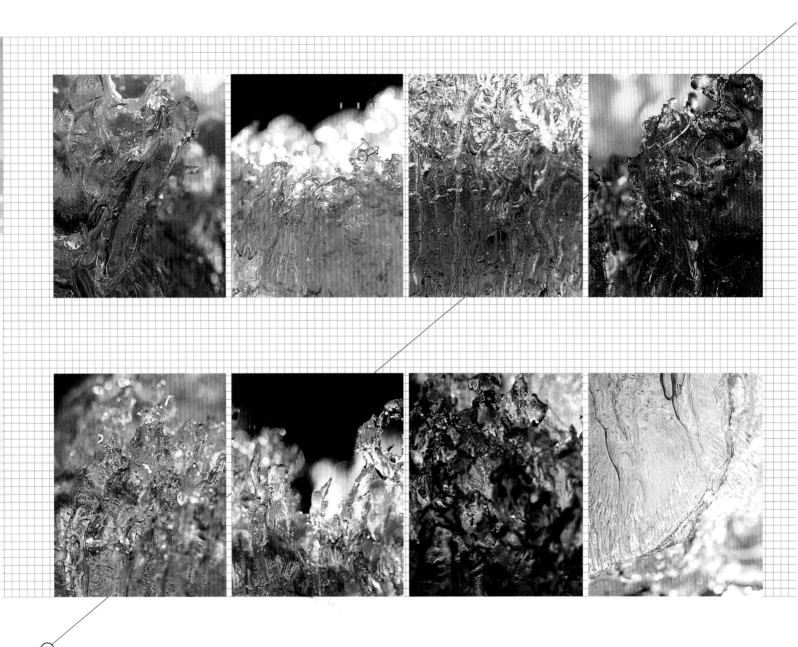

# Project: GTLK

**Designer:** Andrey Muratov;
**Client:** Gosudarstvennaya Transportnaya Lizingovaya Kompaniya | GTLK©;
**Software:** After Effects.

"GTLK" video is created for the National (Gosudarstvennaya) Transportation Leasing Company. The objective is to present the company logo with animation – the sphere. Ice is shot in real time. Its properties and dynamics are served as the process that is able to realize an idea of advertising object. The physical change of ice is taken as a metaphor for movement, captured by camera, identical to the process of melting.

**Project:** Evenescent Beauty

**Design Firm:** caigriffith.com;
**Designer:** Cai Griffith;
**Client:** Personal Project;
**Software:** After Effects, Premiere, Photoshop.

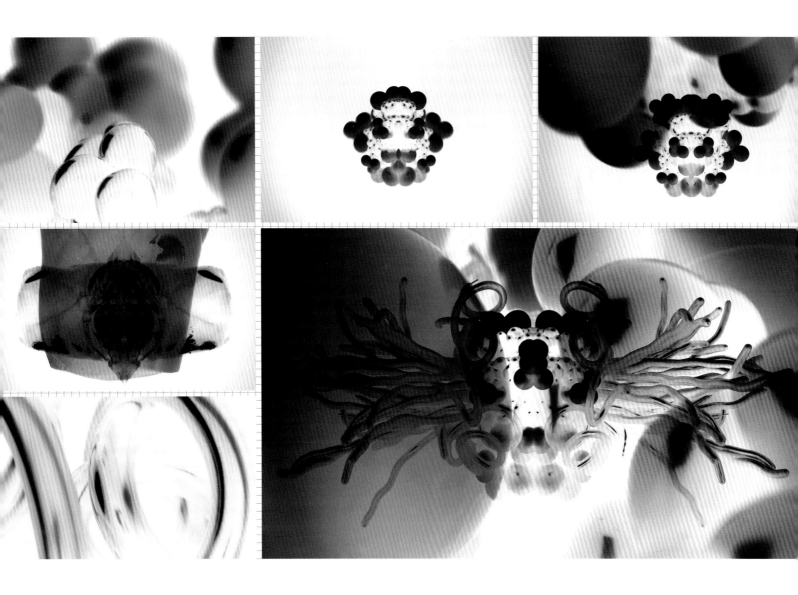

Designed by Cai Griffith, the work Evenescent Beauty is a personal project concerning the creation of something beautiful, and the video in which the fantastic and amazing elements are constantly changed, showing a wonderful visual effect. Special thanks to David Crofts (the balloon modeller) and Cai Griffith for making the project possible.

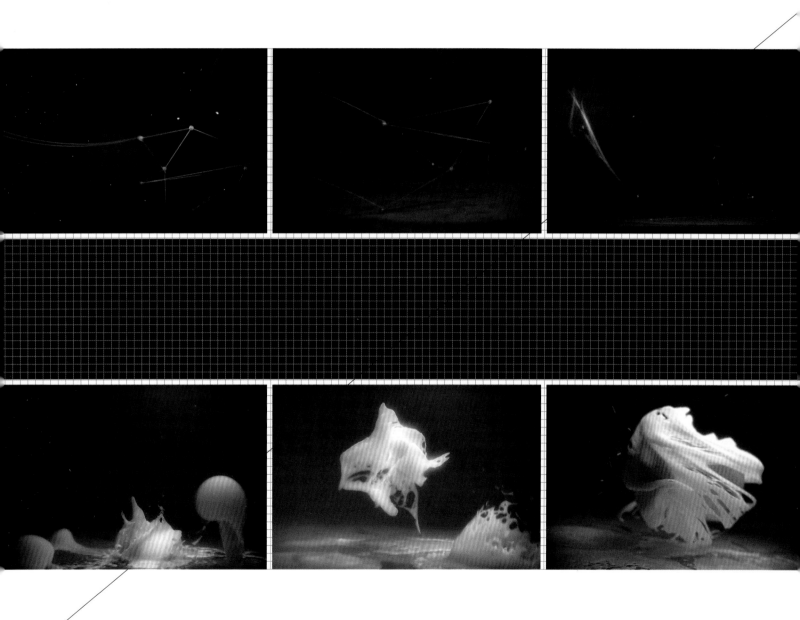

# Project: Nokta

**Design Firm:** Onur Senturk TV;
**Designer:** Onur Senturk;
**Software:** After Effects, 3ds Max, RealFlow, Mud Box.

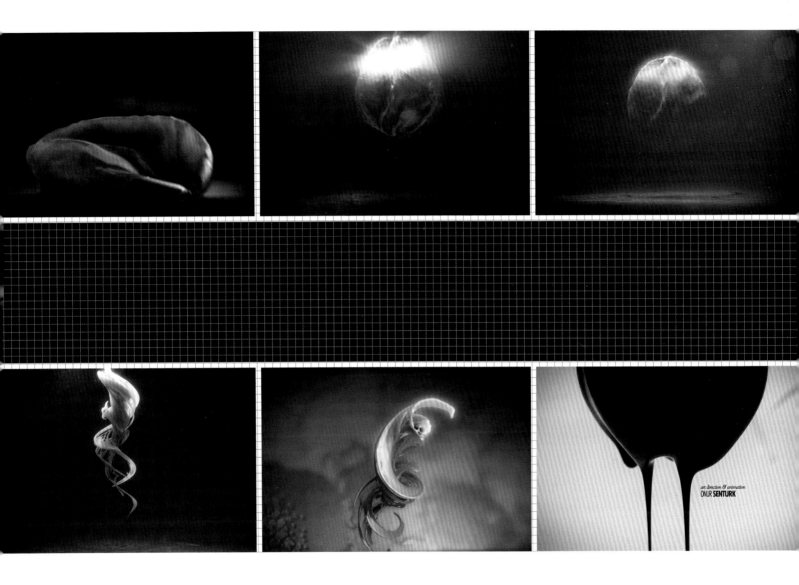

art direction & animation
ONUR SENTURK

Nokta is an abstract short film project with a creative and distinctive style. It is also an improvisation of organic pieces while considering themes like power, control and luck. Using low-budget equipment and with the combination of actual camera shooting, 2D and 3D animation techniques, the film alters the reality to physics of the real world with the help of the liquid and dynamic simulations' impact.

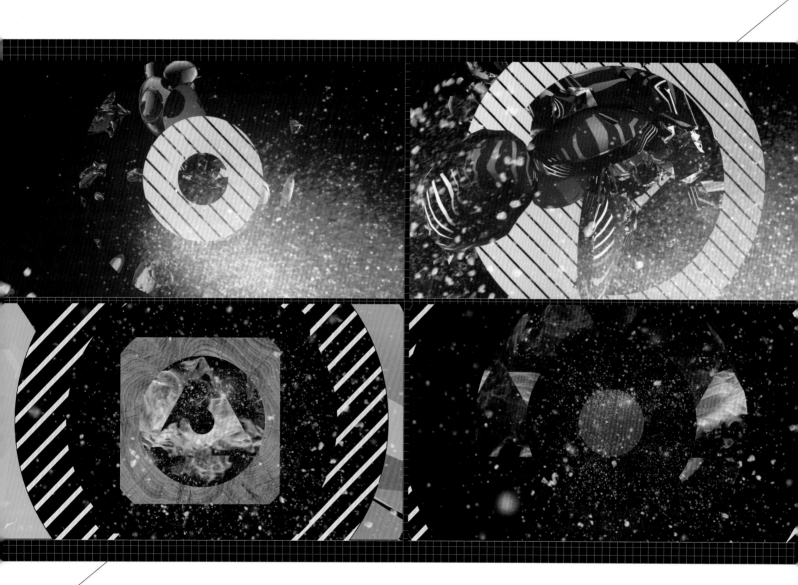

**Project:** OFFF 2011 Year Zero

**Design Firm:** Actop;
**Designers:** Alvaro Posadas & César Pesquera;
**Client:** OFFF Barcelona;
**Software:** Adobe Photoshop, After Effects, Cinema 4D.

The festival OFFF approached Actop and asked for a short piece to promote their 2011 edition. The brief is: Year Zero, Year Alpha. It's time to forget the past and look forward to setting up new rules. The festival voluntarily forgets its past and re-invents itself. A Big Bang is created, a first moment of the creation where everything can happen, using different techniques (3D, photography and graphics) to generate a blank page waiting to be written.

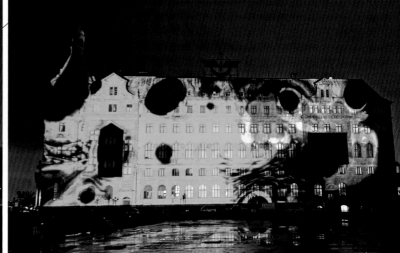

**Project:** Yekpare (monolithic)

**Design Firm:** NERDWORKING;
**Designers:** Candaş Şişman & Deniz Kader;
**Client:** Istanbul 2010 European Capital of Culture Agency;

"Yekpare" is a storyteller who narrates the 8500-year story of Istanbul. The story embraces symbols from the Pagans to the Roman Empire, from the Byzantine Empire to the Latin Empire, and finally from the Ottoman Empire to Istanbul at the present day. The project's conceptual, political and geographical positioning, the location's depth of field and the fact that the entire show can be watched from Kadıköy coast make "Yekpare" a dramatic presentation.

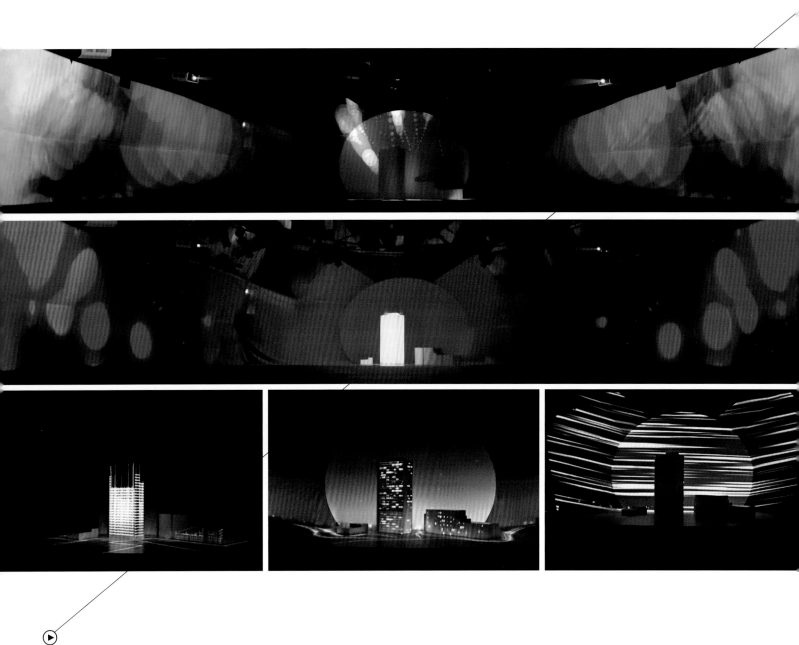

**Project:** NARKULE

**Design Firm:** NERDWORKING;
**Designers:** Candaş Şişman & Deniz Kader;
**Client:** Tepe İnşaat.

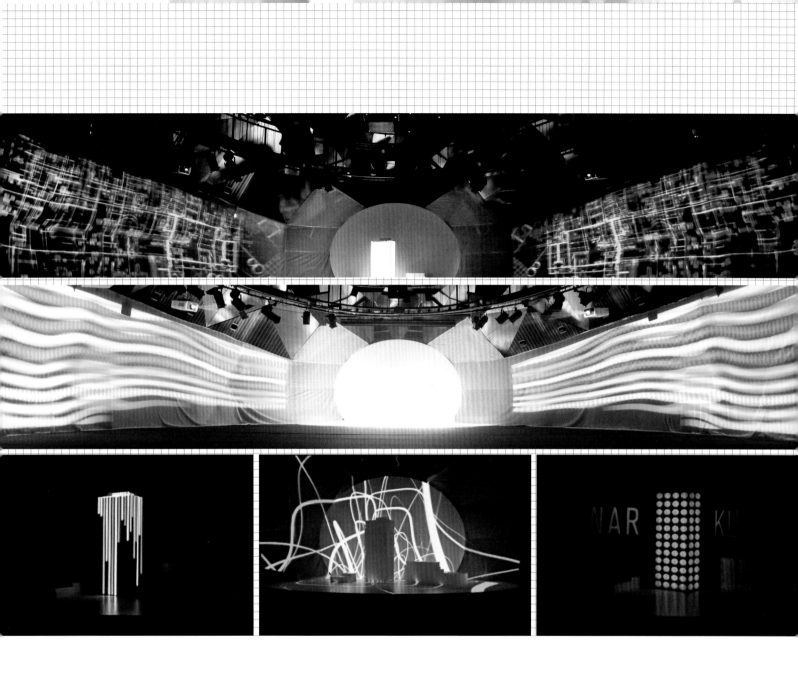

NARKULE is located at the top of Narcity, which is designed by Nevzat Sayın. Their first public housing project has a major public building now. The story of this performance is built on facts behind the curtain, such as energy of life and abstract links of the buildings. The designers covered walls / stage floor / stage background to project visuals on it. The trade center and C Block of Narcity are built by architects as 1/50 models. When synchronize and project visuals on the building, it independently maps 5 different surfaces at the same time.

**Project:** Imagine

**Design Firm:** UNDREAM;
**Designer:** Murat Pak;
**Software:** Cinema 4D & After Effects.

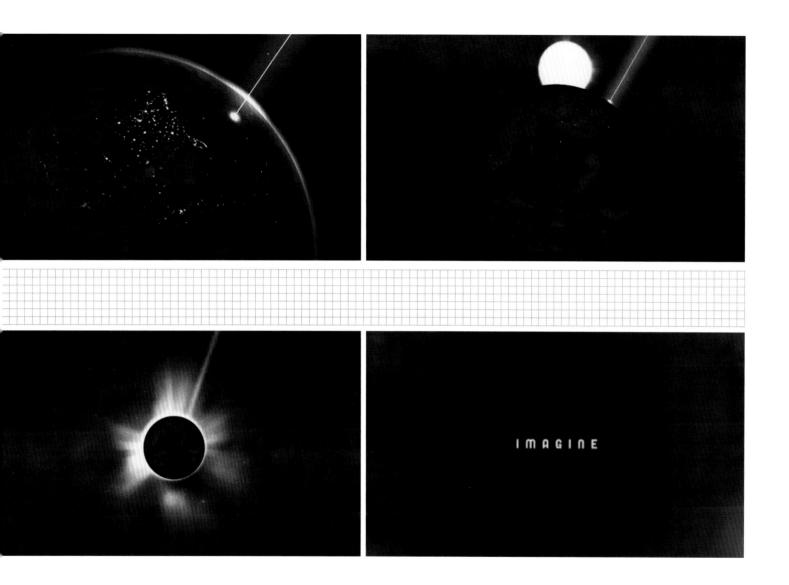

What happens in the thinnest slice of time? Imagine is a project searching for abstract visual metaphors to explain the "moment" of imagination, as it designs a scene where everything is coincidentally happening with a pre-defined connection. The usage of space is a key element of the project, since it is the only size-related variable that changes from scene to scene.

**Project:** Bass Sound Wave Spot Series

**Design Firm:** Maxilla Inc;
**Designer:** Ryunosuke Shimura;
**Software:** After Effects, Premiere, Cinema 4D.

This series of motions are designed for Spots for Bass Sound Wave. Bass Sound Wave is one of the international live streaming media programs of Maxilla.TV. The works are presented by members of the creative team Maxilla and BSW DJ crew.

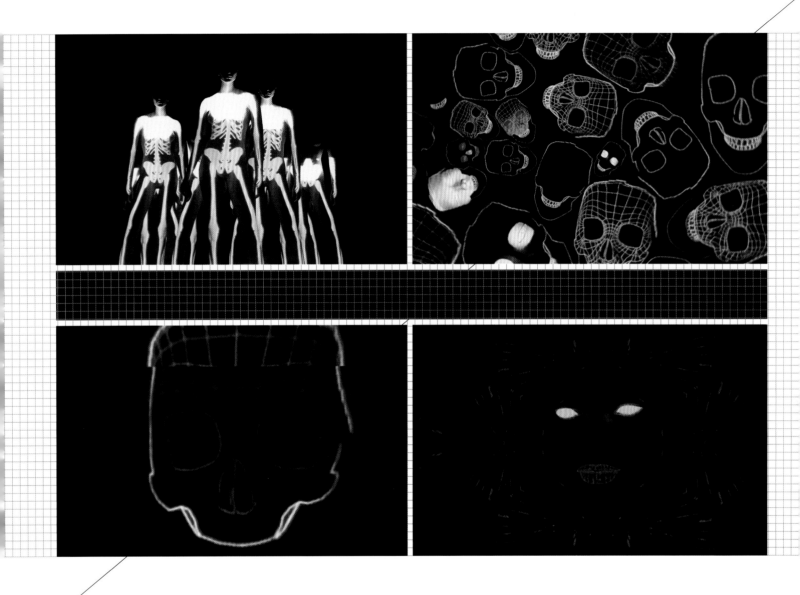

**Project:** Mille – Crysteena

**Designer:** UPPER FIRST;
**Client:** Mille;
**Software:** After Effects, Cinema 4D, Modul8.

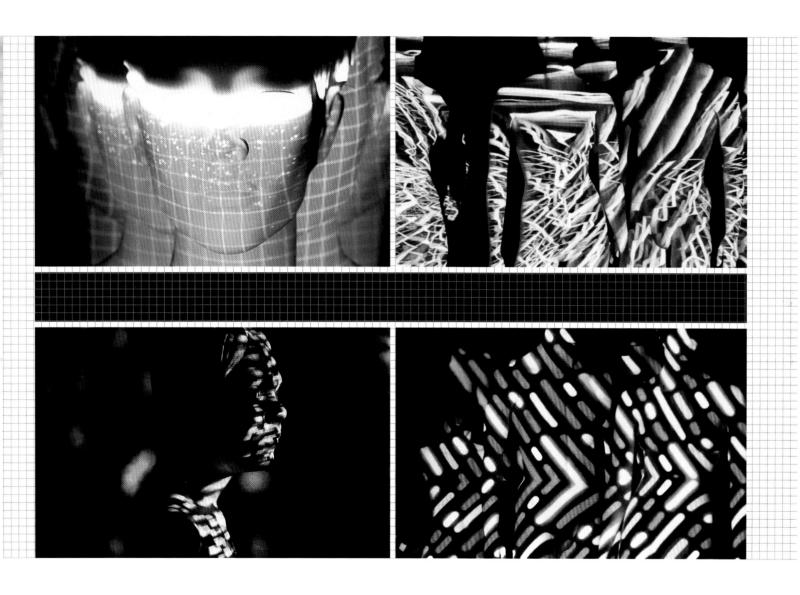

After spending a long night in a dark, creepy warehouse full of mannequins, and many hours of spare time in front of computer, this is the achievement! In this piece, UPPER FIRST combines two of their interests, creative visuals and electro music, to create a music video for the up-and-coming Swedish artist Mille. The idea is to use projections on mannequins to achieve a different and interesting expression where graphics almost become clothes on the bodies.

**Project:** Art Presentation for TTK Company

**Design Firm:** Mercator Group;
**Art-director:** Nonna Khismatullina;
**Executive Producer:** Andrey Skvortsov;
**Client:** TTK Company;
**Software:** After Effects, Premiere, 3ds Max, Photoshop.

Two companies TTK (Russia) and NTT Communication (Japan) joined the project on the Sakhalin-Hokkaido Underwater Cable System installation. This movie was shown at the opening of the conference dedicated to this event. The art presentation is made as the set of little sketches-stories about similarities and differences between Russian culture and Japanese culture.

## Project: MTV 10 x 100

**Design Firm:** MTV Design Services Latam + Hola Mambo;
**Creative Director:** Camilo Barría;
**Directors / Designers:** Camilo Barría, Luis Suarez, Adriana Campos;
**Audio:** Marco Camacho;
**Client:** MTV Networks Latinamerica;
**Software:** After Effects, Cinema 4D, Avidemux2, FFMPEG.

In this short motion design, the end of musical boundaries and genres, the vibrant colors are adopted to create wonderful visual effects. Also a melting-pot of digital creations for drunken analog hearts is presented to celebrate the first 10 years of music from the 21 century.

**Project:** MTV Bicentenario

**Design Firm:** MTV Design Services Latam;
**Creative Directors:** Camilo Barría & Juan Frontini;
**Directors:** Camilo Barría & Anamaría Gutierrez.
**Designers:** Camilo Barría, Gabriel Fermanelli, P. Alfieri, S. Livingstone, Hernán Estevez, Leonardo García;
**Audio:** Avealma Delivery de Sonido;
**Client:** MTV Networks Latinamerica;
**Software:** After Effects, Cinema 4D, 3ds Max, RealFlow, Final Cut.

MTV Bicentenario Project is designed to celebrate the 200th anniversary of the creation of 4 Latin American Countries (Argentina, Colombia, Mexico and Chile). This project is aired from May through September 2010, and includes some other actions on screen like a special programming grid and special interviews with musicians from each country.

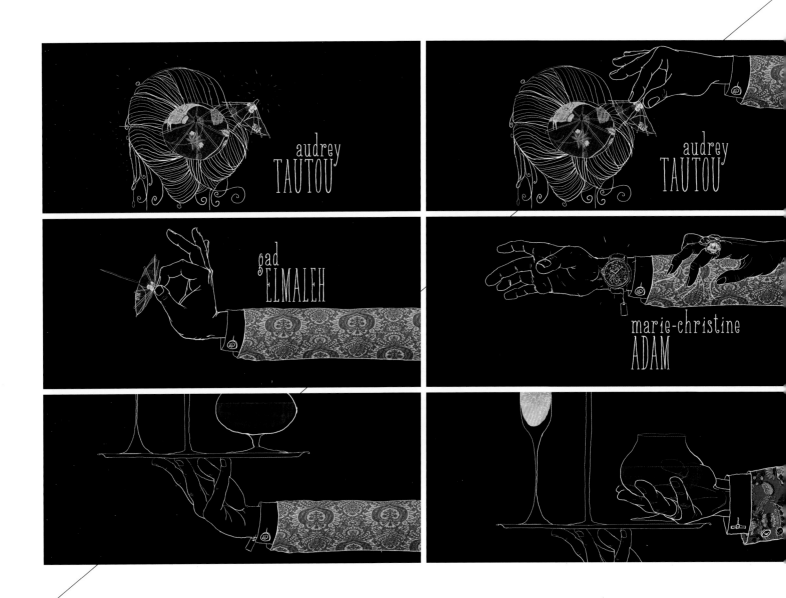

**Project:** Hors de Prix

**Design Firm:** DEUBAL;
**Designers:** Olivier Marquézy & Stéphanie Lelong;
**Client:** Les Films Pelleas ;
**Software:** After Effects, Illustrator, Photoshop.

vernon
DOBTCHEFF

annelise
HESME

Hors de Prix is a romantic comedy by Pierre Salvadori that takes place in the south of France's luxury hotels. The umbrella is a strong element in a scene, and here is a prop. The designers want to tell the place and interactions of these characters by hands only, like "grab", "ask", "give" and "suggest". The light drawings on the black background, with the flat textures of fabrics and liquids, the artistic style sets a high class Riviera mood, and it is specially designed for the purpose to reflect "fragility behind appearance".

**Project:** Structured Type

**Design Firm:** Ryan Brownhill Design;
**Designer:** Ryan Brownhill;
**Software:** After Effects & Cinema 4D.

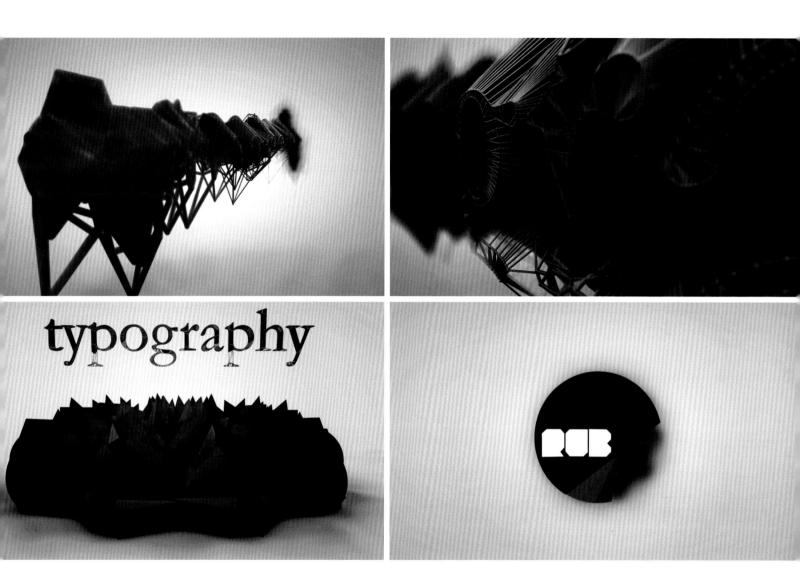

Structured Type is a statement of the advancement in typography due to technology. Old letterpress type had been roughly and slowly growing but because of the advancement in technology, it has helped type grow and aided in the precision and accuracy of its letterforms creating limitless possibilities for type exploration. This piece is created using Cinema 4D and compiling color grad in After Effects.

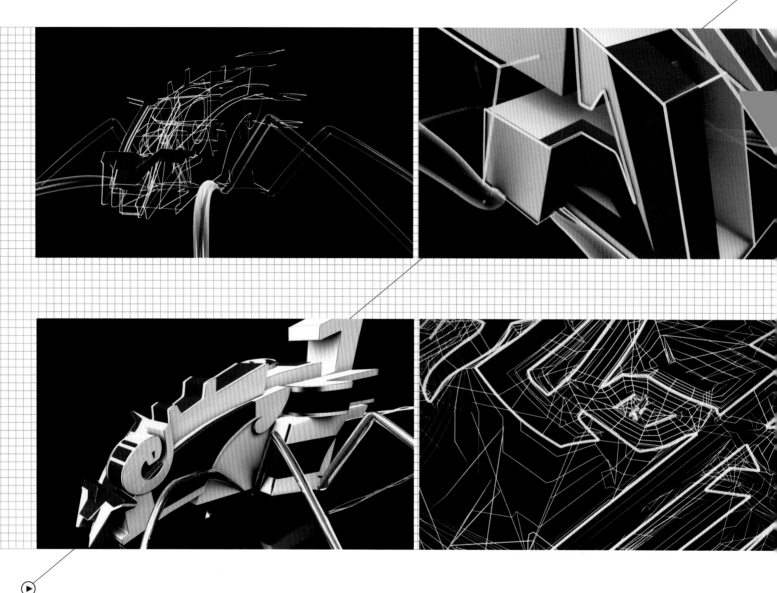

# Project: Makspider

**Design Firm:** Sketchbook Studios;
**Designer:** Mak1one;
**Animation:** Ari Kruger;
**Client:** Mak1one.
**Software:** XSI & After Effects.

This clip is created for the opening of night local graffiti legend Mak1one's exhibition entitled "Kesumo". Mak1one is one of South Africa's most accomplished and respected graffiti artists. Mak supplied Ari Kruger with sketches of the "Makspider" and the designer then modeled in 3D and animated coming to life to the beat of a Humanizer track.

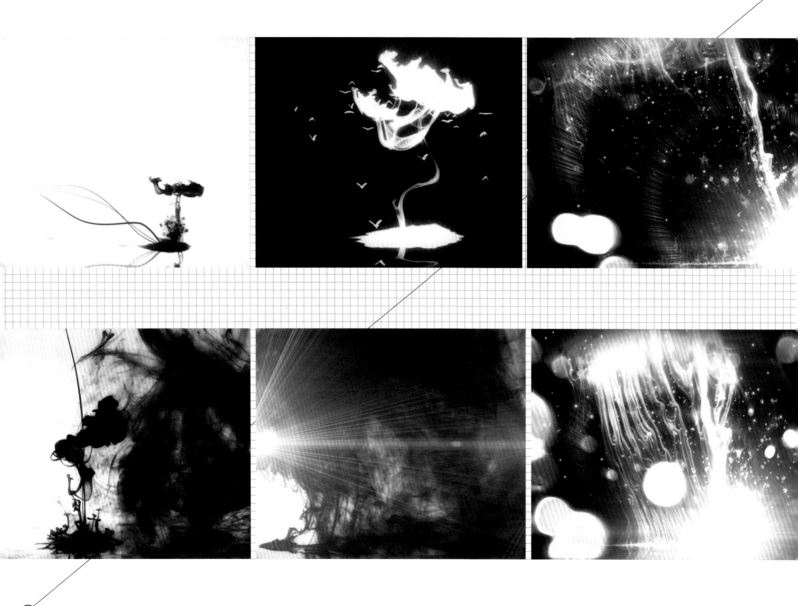

## Project: With Rain

**Design Firm:** TAKCOM;
**Designer:** Takafumi Tsuchiya;
**Client:** Aus;
**Software:** After Effects .

Takafumi Tsuchiya and his team designed this short promo for AUS. Tsuchiya adopted the Japanese "Sumi" ink in the creation of the work. The mix of black and white colors portrays an image of crossing and blending, just like the sound of rain heard outside the window.

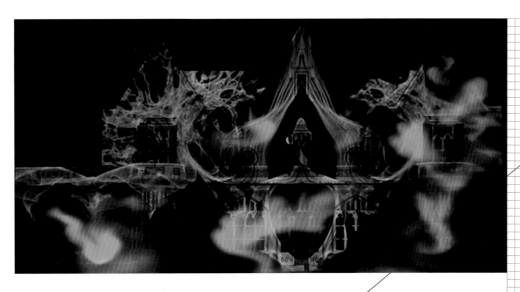

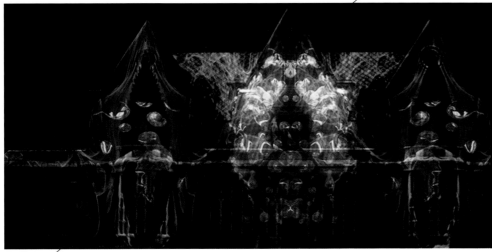

**Project:** "Drone" Large Scale Video Projection on Villa Serra Facade

**Design Firm:** Somatic AV;
**Designers:** Sara Meloni & Giovanni Conti;
**Client:** Municipality of Genoa;
**Software:** VVVV, After Effects, 3ds Max, MSP.

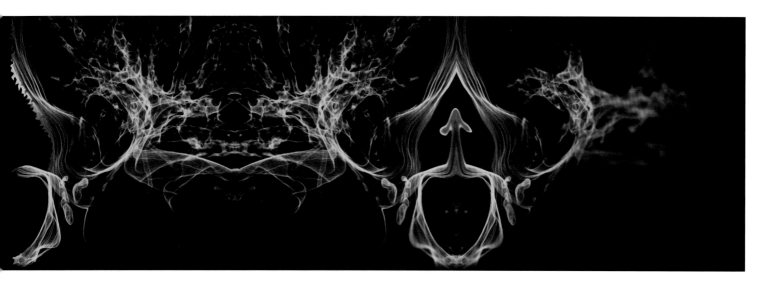

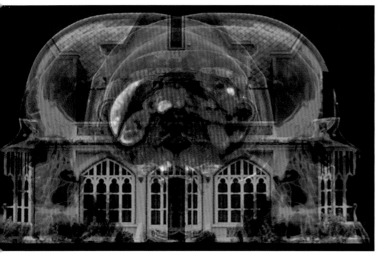 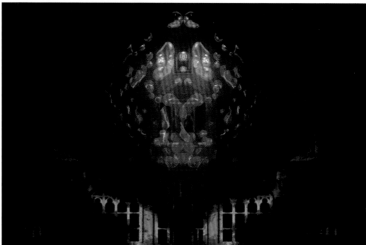

Somatic AV produced for BreakOut festival a sound and dynamic light show, a large scale facade projection designed on purpose for Villa Serra. With images from X-rays, computerized axial tomography and generative visuals as source materials, they shaped a hybrid visual landscape, meeting point for the architectonic language of the Villa and the organic shapes of biological structures. The sensual images and hypnotic synthesized soundscapes transform the physical space of Villa Serra Park mentally, poetically, intimately but shared at the same time.

**Project:** MTV CinePop

**Design Firm:** MTV Design Services Latam;
**Creative Director / Director:** Camilo Barría;
**Designers:** Camilo Barría, Pablo Colabella, Sebastián Ianizzotto;
**Audio:** Santiago Lazarte;
**Client:** MTV Networks Latinamerica;
**Software:** After Effects, Final Cut, Modul8.

This motion design mixes light and surface, time and images all together. That is how the designers reached the basic idea of making movie showings, in which the plus would be the surface where the showings would take place.

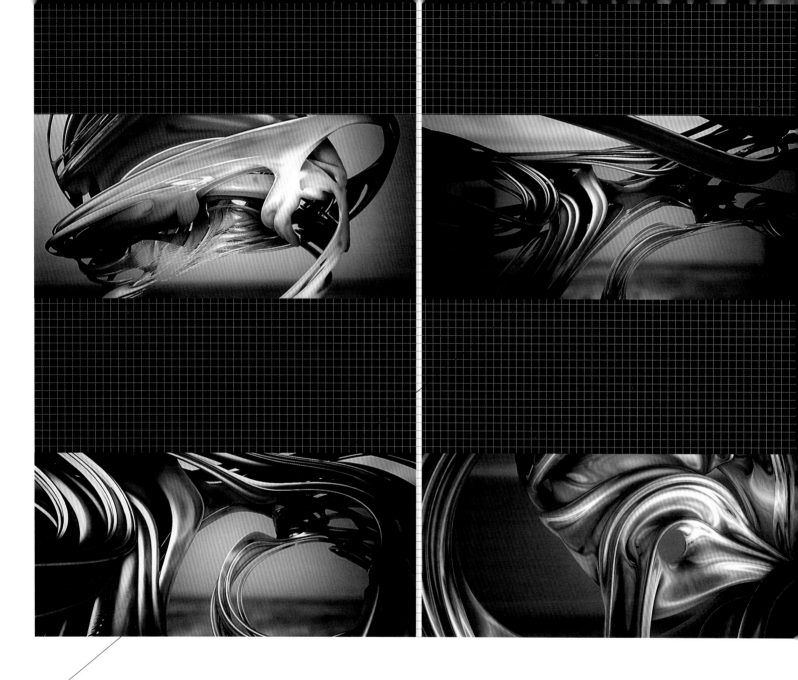

**Project:** Strange Attractors

**Designer:** Nuno Caroço;
**Software:** After Effects & Premiere.

Being a language, mathematics may be used not only to inform but also, among other things, to seduce. After "Julia Rising", this is Nuno Caroço's second project which is based on natural fractals and visual math. He wants to create a passionate form, twisting and rotating to the pulse in the sound of its own existence, evolving to something beautiful, although abstract. All the visual contents are completely generated within After Effects.

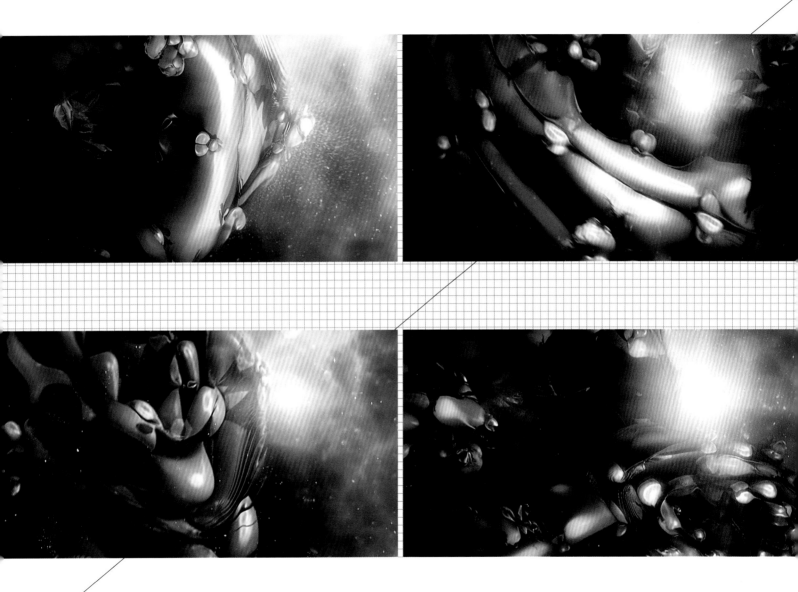

**Project:** Julia Rising

**Designer:** Nuno Caroço;
**Client:** Self-promotion;
**Software:** After Effects & Premiere.

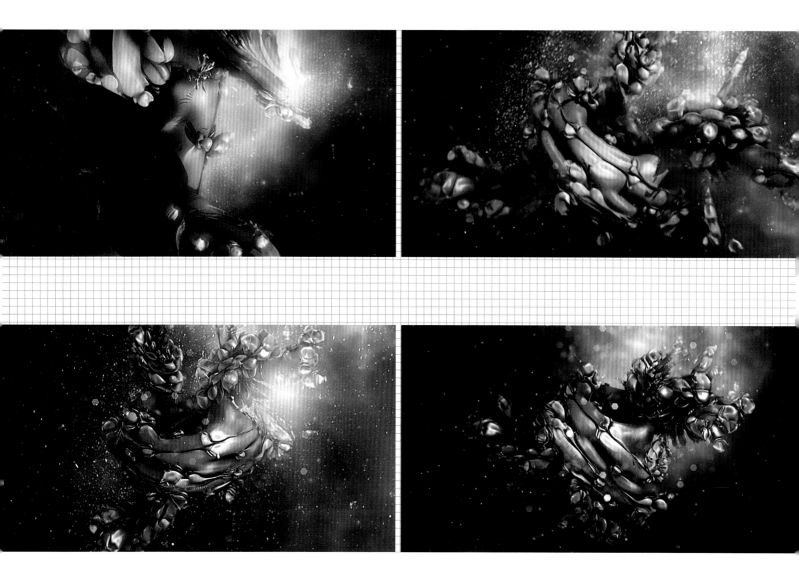

The most beautiful thing we can experience is mystery. After seeing a conference of TED of Benoît Mandelbrot, Nuno is deeply inspired by his speech and the concept of roughness and organic geometry. This work is inspired by natural fractals and patterns of visual math, but in the essence he just wanted to create an emotional piece that translated the beauty of these forms. All the visual contents are completely generated within After Effects.

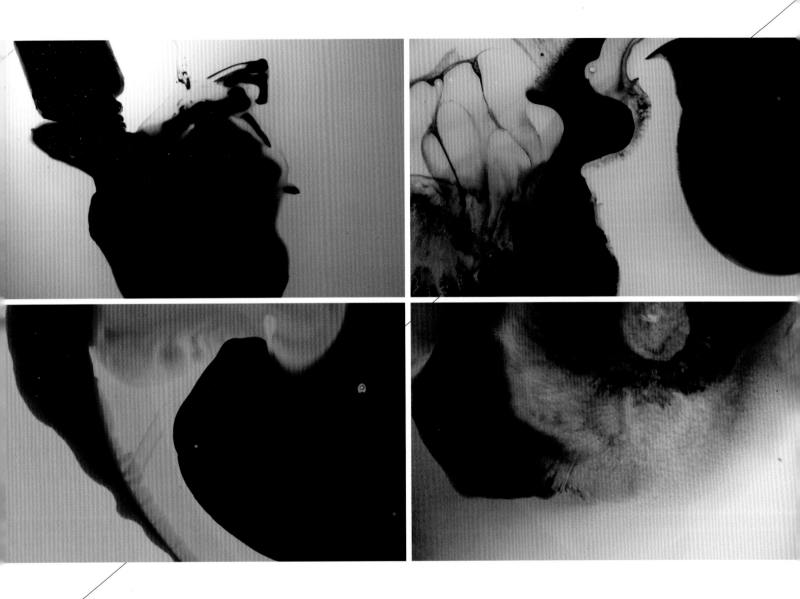

**Project:** Contakt

**Designer:** Joao Lucas;
**Client:** Self-promotion;
**Software:** Adobe Premiere.

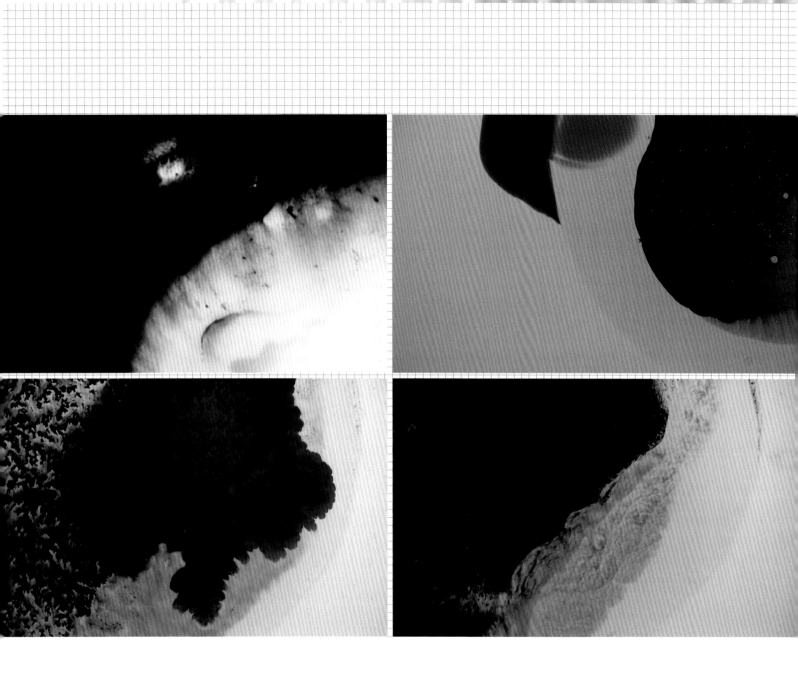

This work is created to do some "exercise" based on the theme: "The transformations that occur in bodies when in touch". The designer just picked his handycam, set it on a small tripod and with a light being the glass of the desk he started to mix some elements like paint, olive oil, shampoo, honey, ink, and basically everything that he thought may have an interesting result. Joao had been shooting the footage for a week, and the most challenging part was the video editing, taking him about 16 hours to finish it.

**Project:** Matchmoving

**Designer:** Joao Lucas;
**Client:** Self-promotion;
**Software:** Lightwave 3D, Boujou, Premiere.

This project is combined by video and 3D. Basically the designer tried to explore different situations and different places, and then put all things together to form an unique final piece. By the time the designer was doing it, he was just trying, failing and learning from it, so in the designer's opinion, this work is the result of those experiments which make his work full of inspiration.

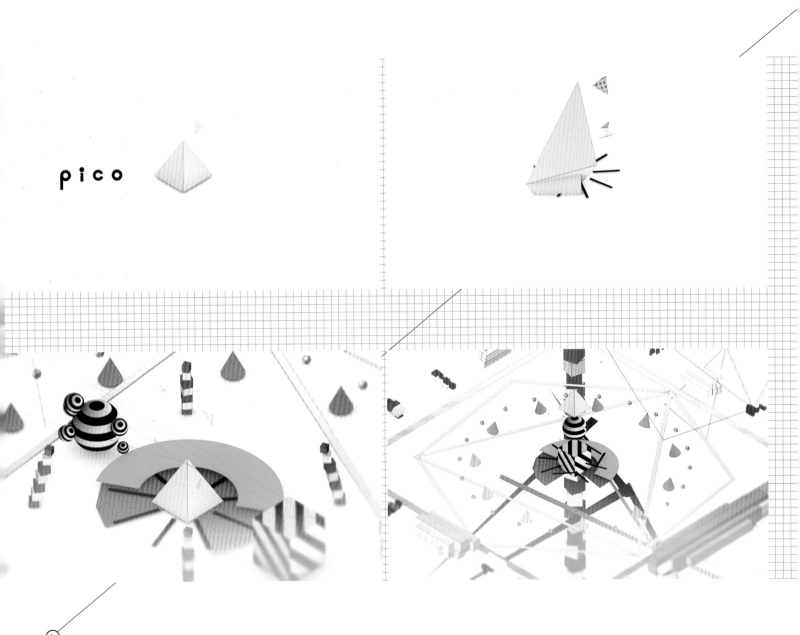

**Project:** Pico

**Design Firm:** TAKCOM;
**Designer:** Takafumi Tsuchiya;
**Client:** SJQ;
**Software:** Cinema 4D & After Effects .

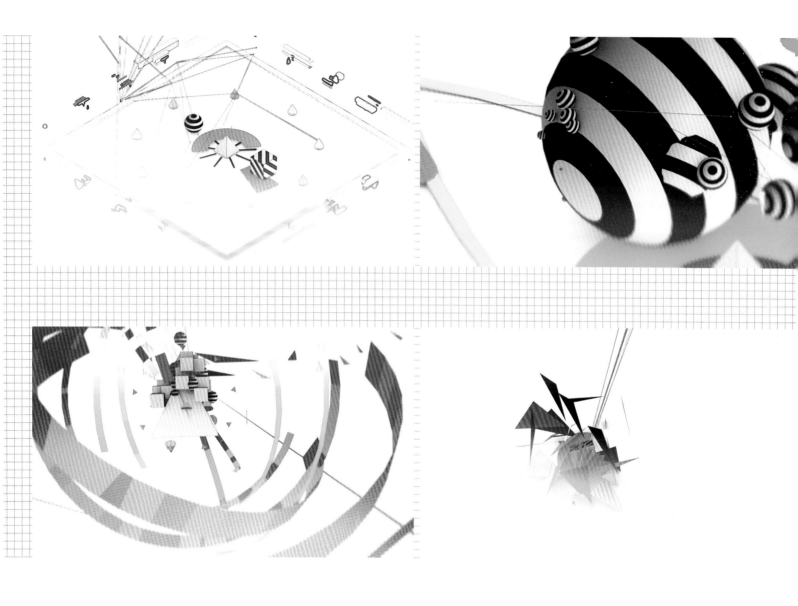

Designed by Takafumi Tsuchiya, this short promo contains some generated visuals which are divided directly from the digital music file from experimental jazz quintet SJQ. Each object in the whole design can represent one sound. These elements are constructed as strange landscapes to create a modern sense.

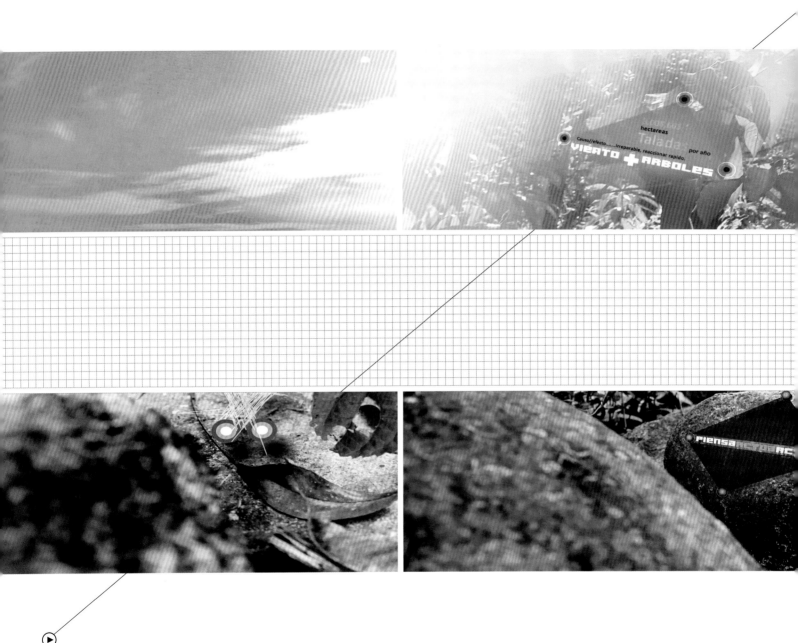

**Project:** En el Silencio

**Design Firm:** MateriaBlanca – Estudio Visual;
**Designer:** Jeison Barba;
**Software:** After Effects, Trapcode Particular v2, Colorista 2, Camera Tracker.

Random shots of a natural environment are the perfect setting for a video attempting to foster ecologic awareness among citizens. Short and clear messages try to find their way into people's minds to help us understand we are all involved in these environmental issues.

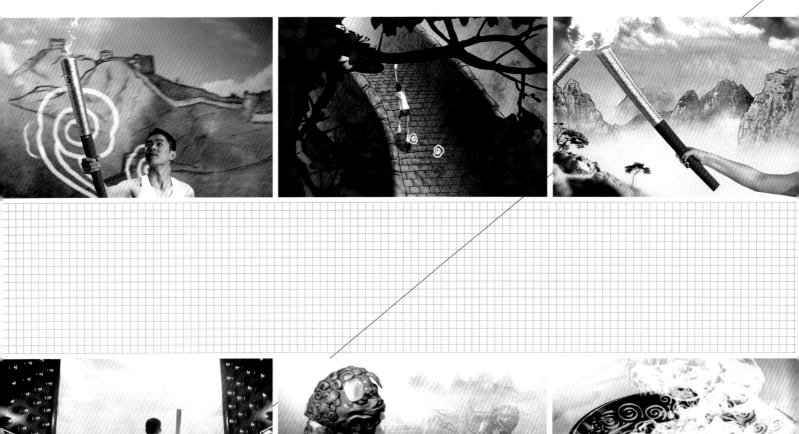

# **Project:** Beijing Olympics

**Design Firm:** RTÉ Graphic Design Department;
**Designers:** Alan Dunne & Alan Eddie;
**Client:** RTÉ Television, Ireland;
**Software:** After Effects, Softimage, Flame.

The concept for the opening title sequence design is to show the arrival of the Olympic torch to a variety of Chinese environments. In the same way that the official logo of the Beijing Olympics is inspired by the rich tradition of calligraphy and paper craft in China, so it is a visual treatment of the design. There is a concerted effort to make the piece quite cinematic with a limited color palette of rich reds and ambers. Each scene is thoroughly researched for visual accuracy and the live action green screen footage is filmed using members of the Chinese community living in Ireland.

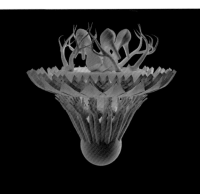

#004/BFA09
BFC *DESIGNER of the YEAR*

#004/BFA09
BFC *DESIGNER of the YEAR*

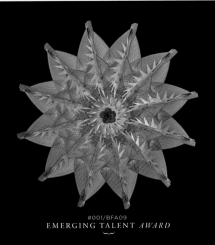

#001/BFA09
EMERGING TALENT *AWARD*

#010/BFA09
ISABELLA BLOW AWARD *for FASHION CREATOR*

## Project: British Fashion Awards

**Design Firm:** ManvsMachine;
**Designers:** Mike Alderson, Tim Swift;
**Animation:** Jon Noorlander, Remi Dessinges;
**Sound Design:** Resonate @ Silent Studios;
**Client:** Swedish Broadcaster;
**Software:** Adobe CS, Maya.

#002/BFA09
ACCESSORY *DESIGNER*

#002/BFA09
ACCESSORY *DESIGNER*

#010/BFA09
ISABELLA BLOW AWARD *for FASHION CREATOR*

#008/BFA09
DESIGNER *BRAND*

A series of bespoke graphic animations are designed to form a nomination package for the prestigious British Fashion Awards ceremony. The live event was held at London's Royal Courts of Justice – inspiring a very British eccentric & architectural approach. All elements are designed specifically for use with Musion Eyeliner 3D holographic projection system, allowing a spectacular 3-dimensional moving life-size hologram to appear within a live stage setting. These animations are part of the entire event brand package, which is created in collaboration with the multi-talented Silent Studios.

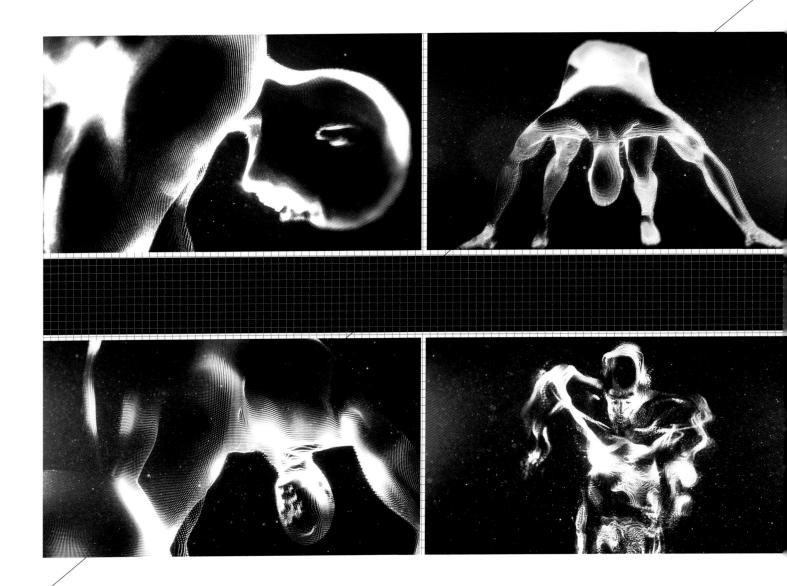

**Project:** Wind is a Part of Me

**Director:** Andrey Muratov;
**Art-Director:** Sergey Golnikov;
**Creative Director:** Viktor Zvegincev;
**Client:** Nike;
**Software:** After Effects.

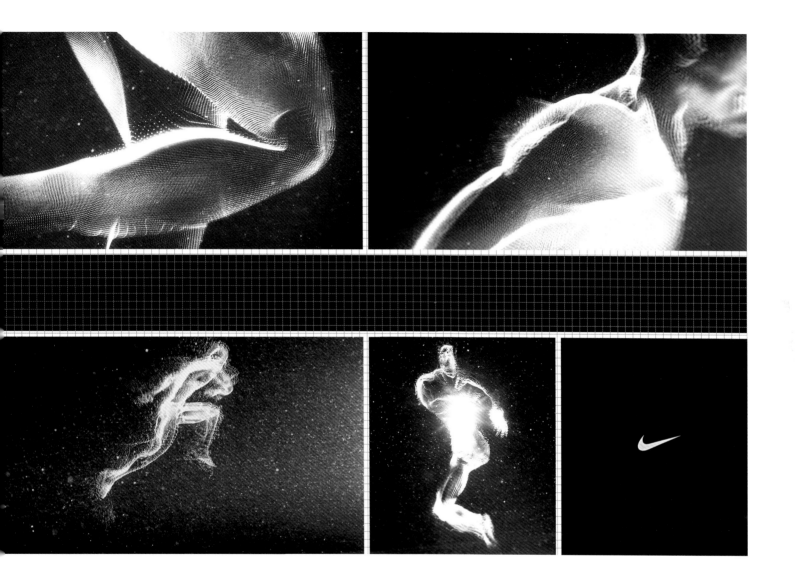

"Wind is a Part of Me" is a work about wind that lives, helps and drives us inside. This design project can be understood as a dynamic comprehension of the concept of a new Nike slogan. The idea of the wind, with its characteristics, is a language that indicates everything is possible with the feasibility of the technological Nike drama.

**Project:** Reel Intro King and Country

**Design Firm:** King and Country;
**Designer:** Sander van Dijk;
**Creative Direction:** King and Country;
**Software:** After Effects & Cinema 4D.

This is a brand promo with the logo presentation of King and Country. A lot of new works have been designed by King and Country, so it is time for a new reel. The designer, Sander van Dijk, created this reel intro for them under the creative direction of Rick Gledhill. In this work, an empty room is filled with some abstract objects which are drawn to match the brand logo perfectly.

**Project:** Tonic

**Design Firm:** MEMOMA;
**Designers:** Hector Hernandez & Daniel Piña;
**Client:** MVS Networks;
**Software:** Photoshop & After Effects.

The Tonic show package is an entertainment program broadcasted by MVS Networks 2010. The city, forest, sky and many other imaginary landscapes are the ideal resource for the development of friendly and funny scenarios. Environments where geometric characters live and give life to awesome situations come and go in funny, incoherent and absurd actions, almost a joke. A King Kong, a UFO, a skier and the city setting on fire! Resources were illustrated by the use of paper and cardboard as raw materials, which combined with stop motion animation and lots of patience results in fresh and graceful movements.

**Project:** Hair Conditioner

**Production:** El.Ei Studios;
**Director:** Jonathan Gurvit;
**Executive Producers:** Sebastián Lopez & Rodrigo Carvajal;
**Software:** 3ds Max, Hairtrix, Combustion, Fusion, Nuke.

VERY PERSONAL LOANS

"Hair Conditioner" is the debut of Jonathan Gurvit, a file director from Argentina. The work won at Cannes Advertising Festival in 2010 and many other international awards. The Santander Río Bank is the leader in loan & mortgage lending. And for this reason, they know very well that for some of their customers, loans & mortgages are actually "VERY PERSONAL". This is the concept that transmits "Hair Conditioner", to be able to have the car that you have always dreamed of and enjoy it your way.

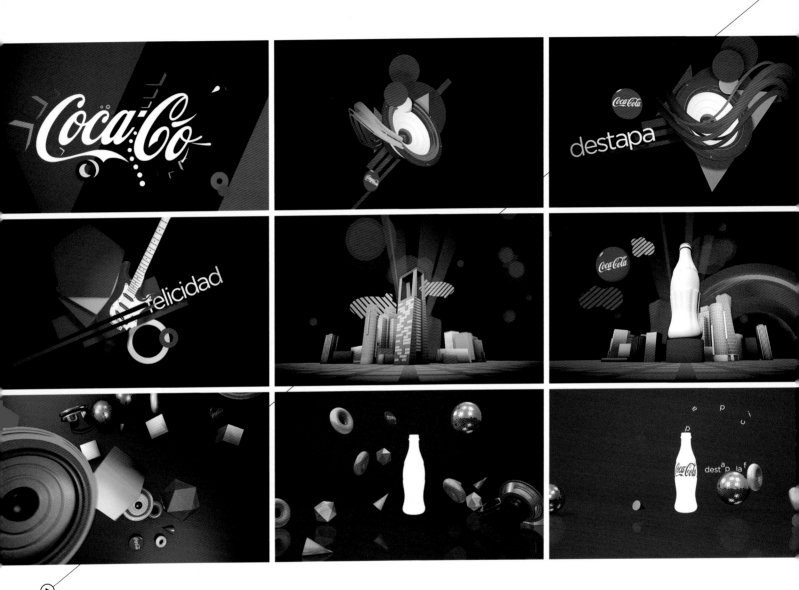

## Project: Coca-Cola Night Visuals 2010

**Design Firm:** Binalogue;
**Concept:** David Carrizales, Marcus Stenbeck,
Alvaro Martín, Lionel Jiménez, Thomas Touron;
**Director:** David Carrizales;
**Client:** The Coca-Cola Company;
**Software:** After Effects, 3ds Max, Maya, Photoshop, Illustrator, Trapcode Suite.

This series of commercial promos – the 2010 night visuals package for 5 brands of the Coca-Cola Company – are conceptualized, directed and developed by Binalogue. The visuals are designed to be displayed throughout Spain during sponsored night events, and the design is based on Coca-Cola's key brand values: open happiness, optimism, originality and authenticity.

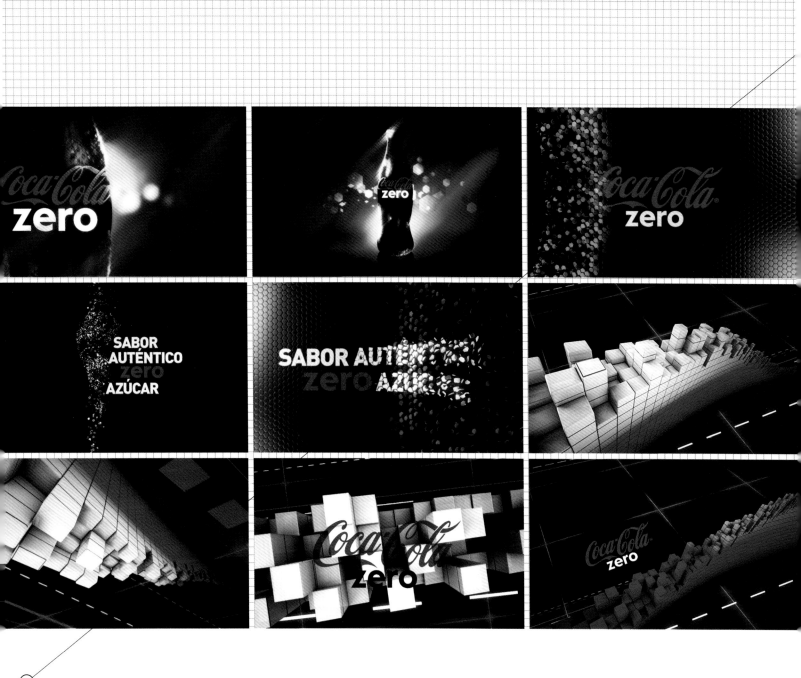

**Project:** Coca-Cola Zero Night Visuals 2010

**Design Firm:** Binalogue;
**Director:** David Carrizales;
**Client:** The Coca-Cola Company;
**Software:** After Effects, Maya, Photoshop, Illustrator, Trapcode Suite.

This is one of the series of commercial promos created by Binalogue for 5 brands of the Coca-Cola Company. And this design is also based on Coca-Cola Zero's key brand values: innovation, connection, confidence with a techy treatment.

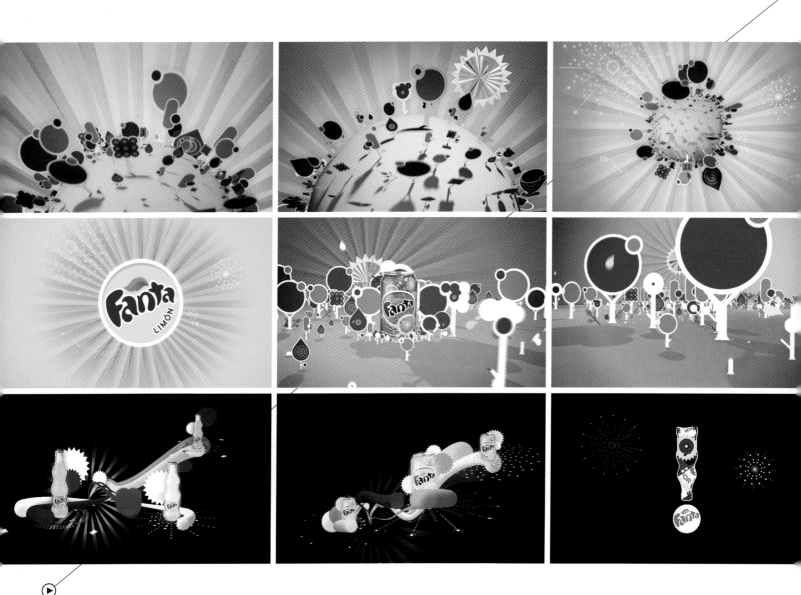

## Project: Fanta Night Visuals 2010

**Design Firm:** Binalogue;
**Concept:** David Carrizales, Marcus Stenbeck,
Alvaro Martín, Lionel Jiménez, Thomas Touron;
**Director:** David Carrizales;
**Client:** The Coca-Cola Company;
**Software:** After Effects, 3ds Max, Photoshop, Illustrator, Trapcode Suite.

This is another work from the series of commercial promos created by Binalogue for 5 brands of the Coca-Cola Company. Aiming at a teenage target audience, this set of visuals are also designed to be displayed throughout Spain during sponsored night events.

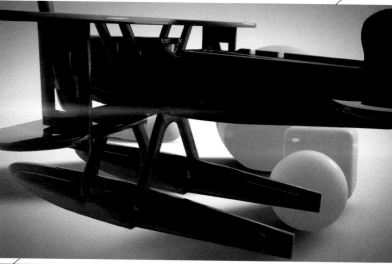

# Project: ONIX Toy ID

**Design Firm:** ONIX – motion stuff;
**Designer:** Leonardo Rica;
**Client:** ONIX – motion stuff;
**Software:** After Effects & Cinema 4D.

With a playful touch and some 3D dynamics, this design idea is to create a fresh, glossy and minimal ID that represents the attitude and beliefs of ONIX, a company that prefers great and well-handled simple ideas to a complex non-conceptual work. The project is made in Cinema 4D, mixing primitive elements with a detailed glossy toy plane, finished in After Effects for the edition, flares, and color correction.

**Project:** Smart Extras

**Design Firm:** UPPER FIRST;
**Client:** Sony Ericsson;
**Software:** Nuke, Maya, After Effects, Photoshop.

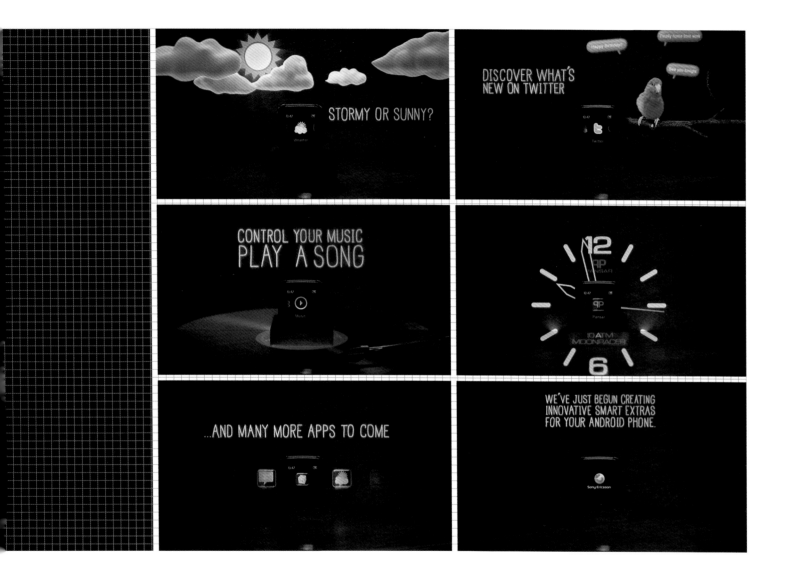

Sony Ericsson approached UPPER FIRST to create a promotional show at the Mobile World Congress in Barcelona. The client wanted a film presenting their new concept of Smart Extras with the mini display LiveView in focus. Smart Extras is a range of phone accessories which were made by adding applications to them. Just as you extend the capabilities of your smart phone with applications, you can now do the same thing with your accessories. This combination of hardware and software sparked an idea about combining a lot of different techniques for an interesting and inspiring look.

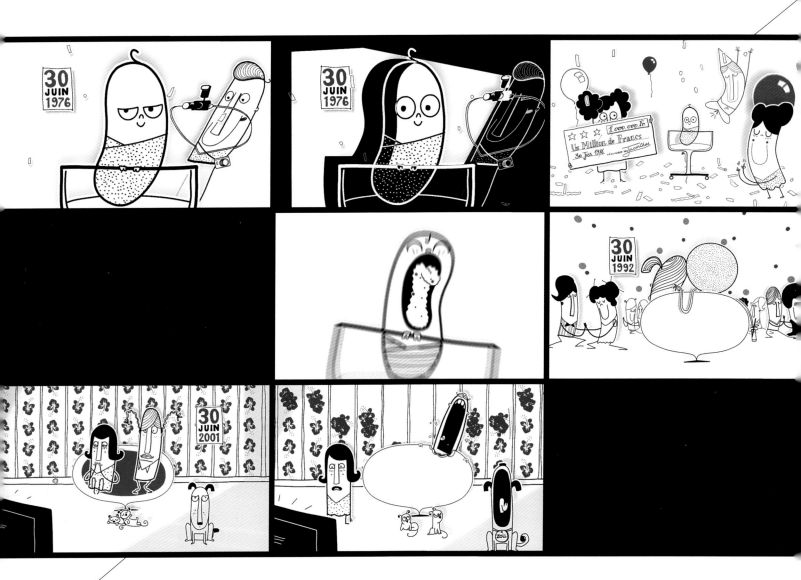

**Project:** FIAT – le cri

**Designers:** Olivier Lescot, Quentin Baillieux, Nicolas Dubois, Lucie Arnissolle;
**Client:** FIAT;
**Software:** Flash & After Effects.

Leo Burnett called on Olivier Marquezy, represented by WIZZdesign°, to direct their latest FIAT film, as part of FIAT's promotional Bonus campaign. The films are based on the personal drawings of Olivier Marquezy. The original creation is done in felt-tip pens on paper and directly animated with Flash. Shadows and cut-off effects are created with After Effects. As a result, the animations have an original, truly creative slant and the characters stem directly from Olivier Marquezy's personal fantasy world.

**Project:** Koerich Technologic Birds

**Design Firm:** Cafundó Estúdio;
**Designer:** Gustavo Brazzalle;
**Client:** Koerich;
**Software:** 3ds Max, Vray, Photoshop, After Effects.

Campaign for Koerich Stores represents the capacity of Technologic Birds in converting old cell phones to all new modern ones. To reach the anticipative goal, Cafundó Estúdio took this commercial promotion and designed this Ad for all Koerich new modern cell phones.

makes people talk

**Project:** Lakerol Xtreme

**Design Firm:** UPPER FIRST;
**Client:** LEAF;
**Software:** After Effects, Nuke, Maya.

This short commercial promo is designed for the product – Lakerol Xtreme of LEAF. Agency Eight Communications are responsible for taking the Lakerol extreme brand further this year and approached UPPER FIRST with the mission to create a series of commercials and billboards. This promo literally launches the first one in the line-up, Lakerol Xtreme.

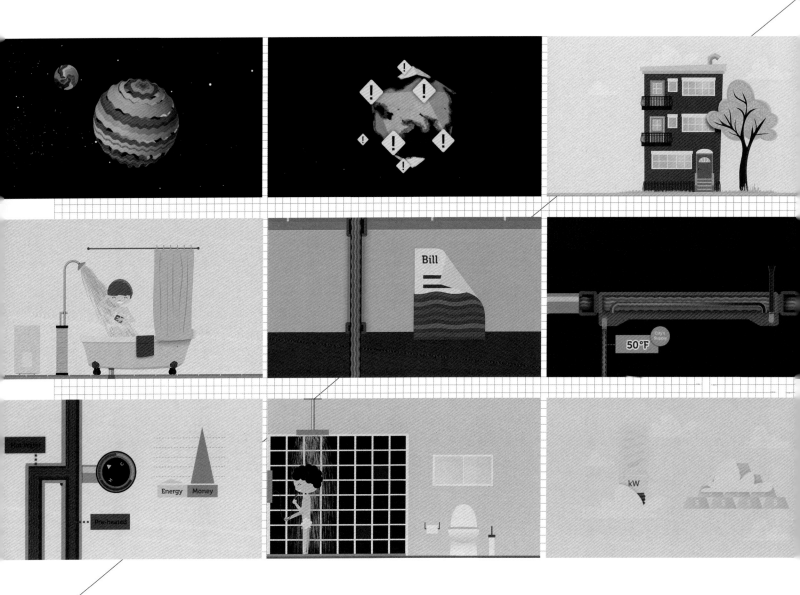

# Project: Ecodrains

**Designer:** Benoit Massé;
**Client:** Prodigy Energy Recovery System;
**Software:** After Effects, Illustrator, Photoshop.

This motion graphic aims to explain how the Ecodrain product works. It's a system that uses wastewater to preheat the cold water, so less energy is needed to take a hot shower. The brief of the designer is to deliver something funny to watch and not too technical.

# Project: Mutlu Akü

**Design Firm:** Mica;
**Directors / Designers:** Luca & Sinem;
**Client:** Mutlu Akü;
**Software:** Maya & After Effects.

In this animated commercial film, a happy accumulator world was designed for the product Mutlu Akü. In Turkish, the name "Mutlu" means happiness. The client wanted to stress durability and happiness with a mascot for their product. In order to express this goal, Luca & Sinem designed a world full of these happy characters which also have durability during the year.

**Project:** MTV the Supercharts

**Design Firm:** UPPER FIRST;
**Client:** MTV Nordic;
**Software:** After Effects, Nuke, Maya, Photoshop.

The Supercharts show is about what's hot on the internet right now and what's searched for the most. This project is designed by UPPER FIRST. The designers worked closely with their friends at MTV in coming up with these ideas and went on to produce it all in record time. They just love these kinds of projects in which they can really let loose and the works that make people go "whaaat?".

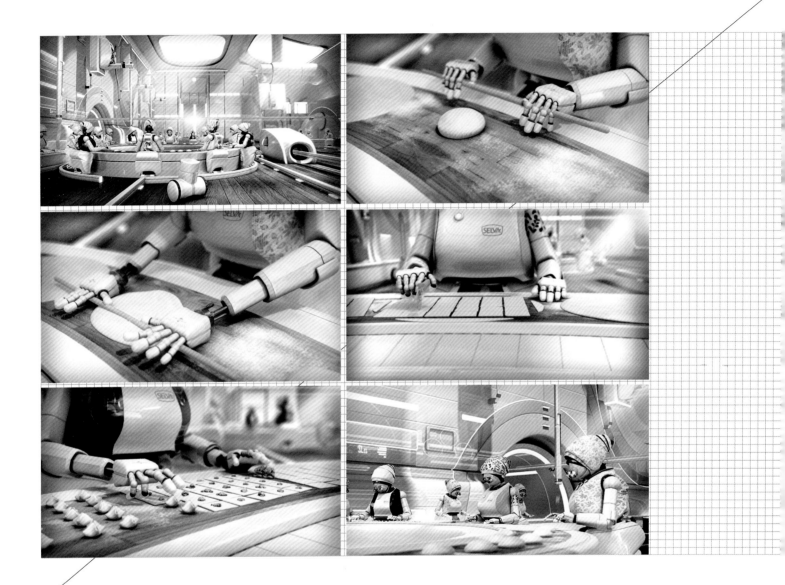

**Project:** SELVA Anatolian Flavour

**Design Firm:** Mica;
**Directors / Designers:** Luca & Sinem;
**Client:** Genna Marketing Communication Group;
**Software:** Maya, After Effects, Photoshop.

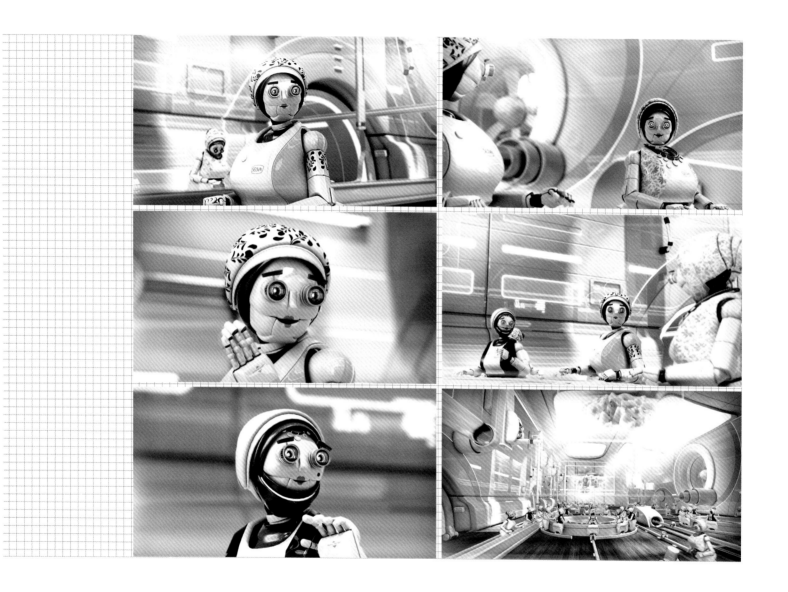

In this animated commercial film, the client wanted to give the message of the traditional handmade macaroni produced with the art technology. The brief of the agency is to create an ironic film around these robotic Anatolian women in a futuristic factory in order to give the message. The most challenging part of this project is the design process of the futuristic robot characters which are related to traditional Anatolian women. According to the client brief, the futuristic factory is designed with a clean look and warm colors to comply with the visual identity of food brand.

**Project:** Sky High

**Design Firms:** Eugene and Louise / Birg and The Fridge;
**Client:** Marble Sounds;
**Software:** Illustrator, Photoshop, Cinema 4D, After Effects, Final Cut Pro.

Sky High is an animated music promo for the band Marble Sounds. It takes us on a trip through the mindset of a lonely lumberjack. The music video revolves around a man who lives isolated in his cabin in the woods. Overpowered by his solitude, the lonely man tries to build a perfect and imaginative world with the memories he has left from better times. One day a magical creature comes to visit him and lures him into this imaginative world to show him that the only way he can be truly happy and free is to let go.

**Project:** Flying Broom Women's Film Festival 2010

**Directors / Designers:** Deniz Kader & Candaş Şişman;
**Client:** Flying Broom Women's Film Festival;
**Software:** 3ds Max & After Effects.

The main theme of the festival is "evil". The Festival draws attention to the evils attributed to women. The designers tried to describe this social restraint with black typographical words and give this emotion with criminal feelings. In the animation, you can see some of the words are said to women by society such as "witch", "characterless" and "enticing".

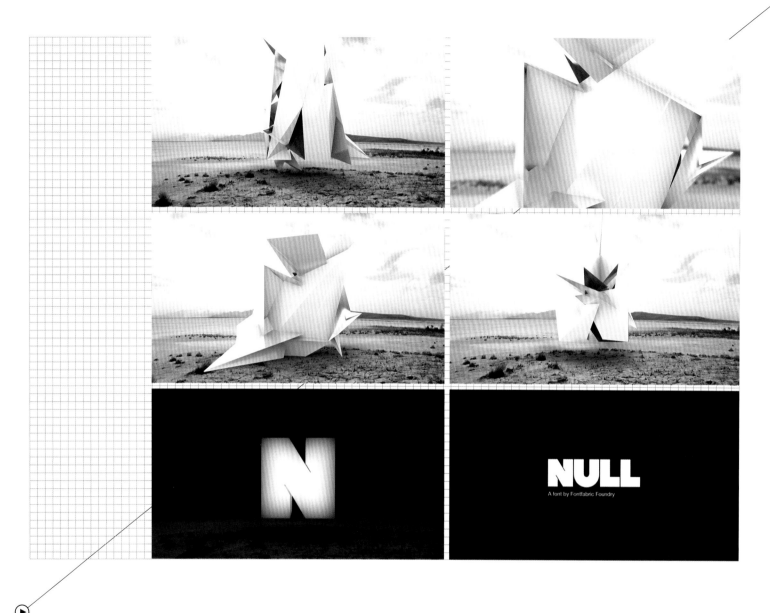

# Project: Null

**Design Firm:** DI-T;
**Designer:** Dimo Trifonov;
**Client:** Fontfabric;
**Software:** After Effects & Cinema 4D.

This is a promotional short motion for a font made by Fontfabric foundry. This design is a successful try to visualize the font by the expression of the gradually changed paper folding. It turns to the letter "N" at last, which emphasizes the letter "N" in the word "Null". From the idea, 3D Animation, to post production, Dimo Trifonov takes charge of the whole process.

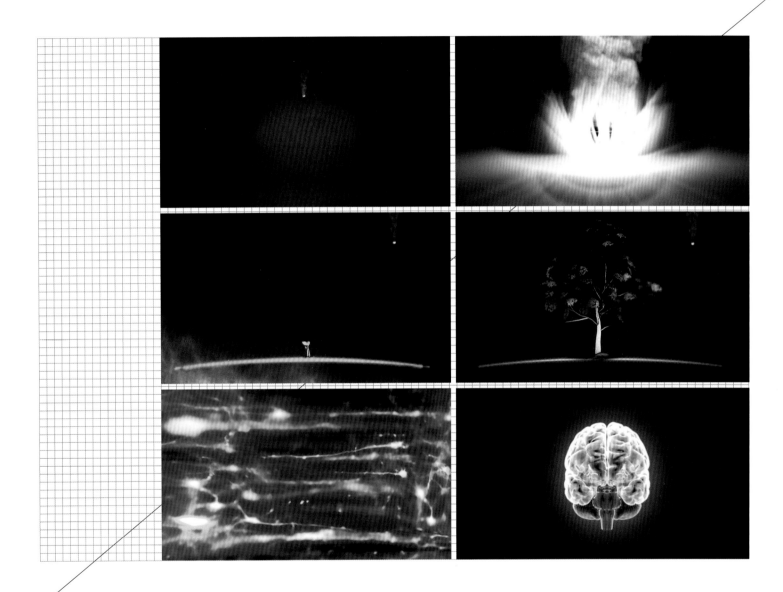

# Project: The Seed

**Designer:** Nate Londa;
**Client:** Savannah College of
Art & Design;
**Software:** After Effects & Cinema 4D.

The seed is a very powerful symbol. To briefly sum it up, perhaps a seed is a singularity and thus a gateway to a singularity. Plant a seed, and a tree will grow. Within that tree will grow birds, insects, and oxygen. A universe will exist within a tree, and all of this comes from a seed. The designer wanted to portray the idea of sharing knowledge in an abstract, almost unrecognizable fashion. The seed is the basis of life, the basis of an idea. It can be planted and dispersed, spreading life and ideas. One tiny idea can create an infinite amount of ideas.

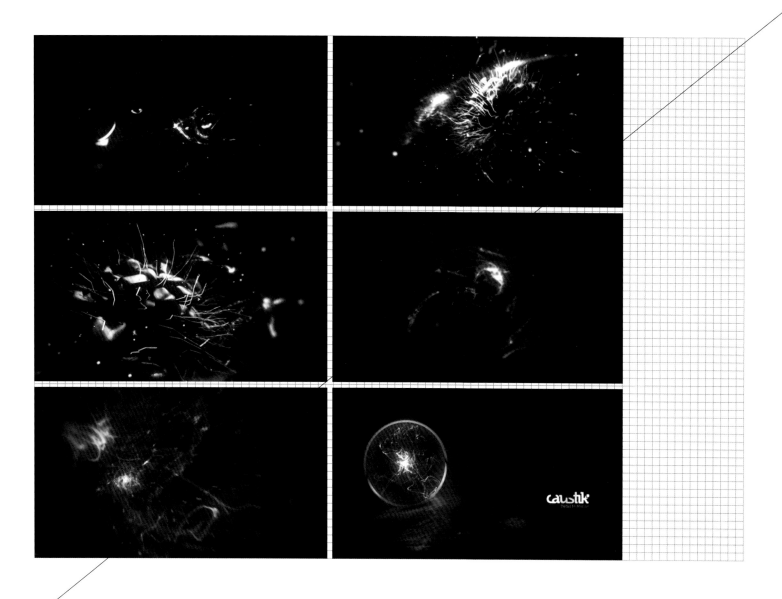

**Project:** Caustik | Detail in Motion

**Design Firm:** Caustik LLC;
**Designer:** Amine Alameddine;
**Software:** 3ds Max, Particle Flow, After Effects.

This piece is a brand promo for the design team Caustik LLC. It is a tribute to Pierre Magnol. It's an adapted variation of an original piece entitled Nano Design by Gkaster. As abstract as it is, it represents well the ideals of the firm (Detail in Motion). Tiny cells and particles are moving, morphing, evolving in a harsh environment. It's a simple smooth form on the outside (the ball) but a complex structure with all its details to sustain it on the inside.

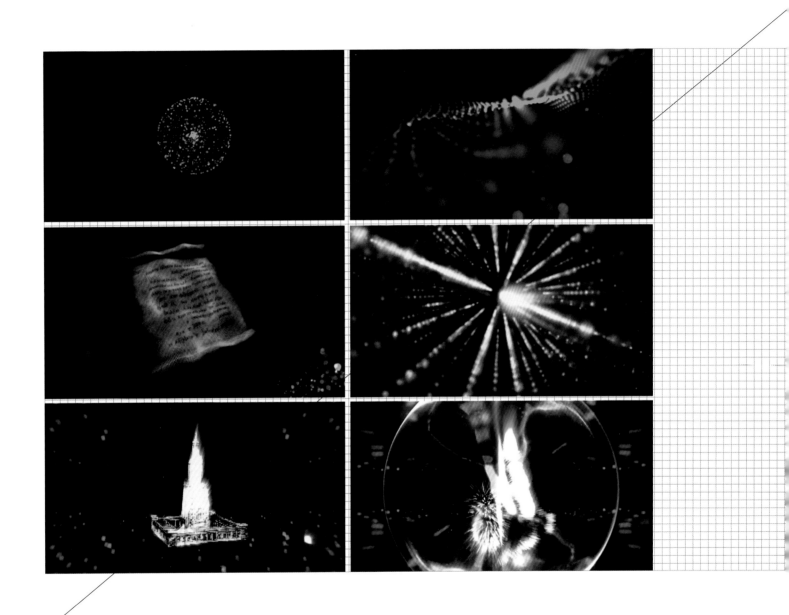

**Project:** ISE, Information Science & Engineering

**Client:** Hochschule Darmstadt;
**Designer:** Frank Sauer;
**Software:** After Effects.

The University of Applied Sciences Darmstadt offers a study called "Information Science and Engineering". Frank Sauer is asked to promote the study in an innovative and interesting way to the upcoming students. Their goal is to create an abstract and endless digital world of information that needs to be organized. The viewer is asked to become one of the new librarians to create order out of chaos to make information and knowledge accessible to mankind. The spot is completely done in After Effects using the additional Plug-In Trapcode Particular and Trapcode Form.

SIMPLER iS BETTER

**Project:** 7UP

**Design Firm:** WIZZdesign°;
**Designer:** Olivier Marquezy;
**Client:** 7UP;
**Software:** After Effects & Flash.

This motion design includes five little scenes exposing interactions between Mr. Green and Mr. Yellow, who have many ways to melt together, figuring the mix of lemon and lime, in a dynamic and bubbly way. This set is voluntarily very simple and graphic, using white backgrounds, sharp designs and plain colors. The attention is focused on the action, which always leads to the disintegration and melting of the two characters, Mr. Green and Mr. Yellow, transformed into bubbles.

# Project: World Expo – Happy Street

**Design Firm:** PlusOne;
**Designers:** Martijn Hogenkamp & Tim van der Wiel;
**Client:** Sogeo;
**Software:** After Effects, Photoshop, Illustrator, 3ds Max.

This short promo is an animation created for the Dutch pavilion, which is called happy street, at the Shanghai World Expo 2010. Happy Street is a complete street in the shape of an eight, a lucky number to the Chinese, and stands out in particular because of its striking, playful, and very open design. Körmeling developed an ideal city in a roller coaster construction.

# Project: Caballero

**Designers:** Carlo Vega & Adam Gault;
**Client:** Victor Caballero & Bleu Blanc Rouge;
**Software:** After Effects & Photoshop.

This short commercial promo was designed for Victor Caballero and Bleu Blanc Rouge. The designers adopted yellow as the basic color and palette environment that present the origin and richness of the wine successfully.

**Project:** Amsterdam Osdorp

**Design Firm:** PlusOne;
**Designers:** Martijn Hogenkamp, Tim van der Wiel, Elias Widerdal;
**Client:** Amsterdam Osdorp;
**Software:** After Effects, Photoshop, Illustrator, 3ds Max, Cinema 4D, RealFlow.

The city district Amsterdam Osdorp merged with Slotervaart and Geuzenveld-Slotermeer, and is given the name Amsterdam Nieuw-West. This change also means the end of 20 years of restructuring urbanized areas. PlusOne is asked to create an intriguing video, featuring the buildings they find most characteristic. Restructuring urbanized areas isn't all about aesthetics. That is why they chose to put emphasis on the architects and especially its inhabitants and the surroundings of the buildings. To achieve this, they decided to combine live action video with 2D and 3D animation.

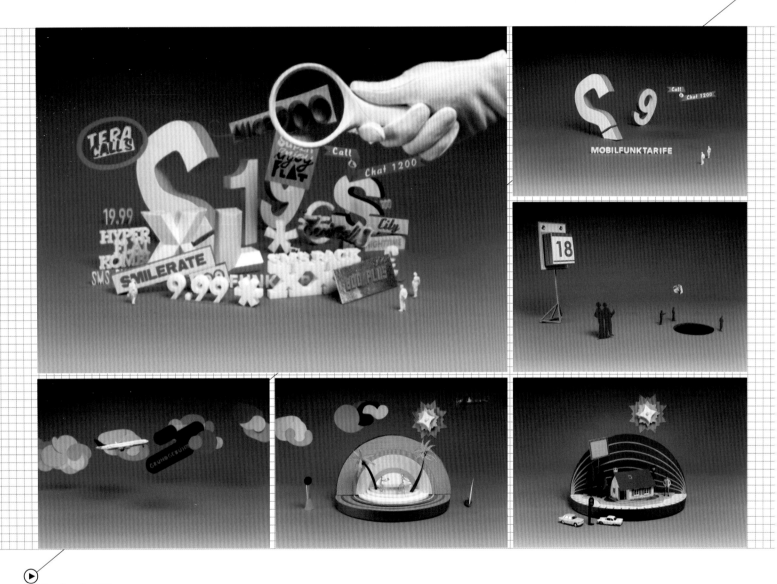

## Project: O2o

**Design Firm:** Parasol Island;
**Director:** Moustache (Hugo Ramirez & Olivier Patté);
**Head of Design:** Charles Bals;
**Producers:** Viola Habermehl & Philip Hansen;
**Client:** O2;
**Software:** Dragon Stop Motion & After Effects.

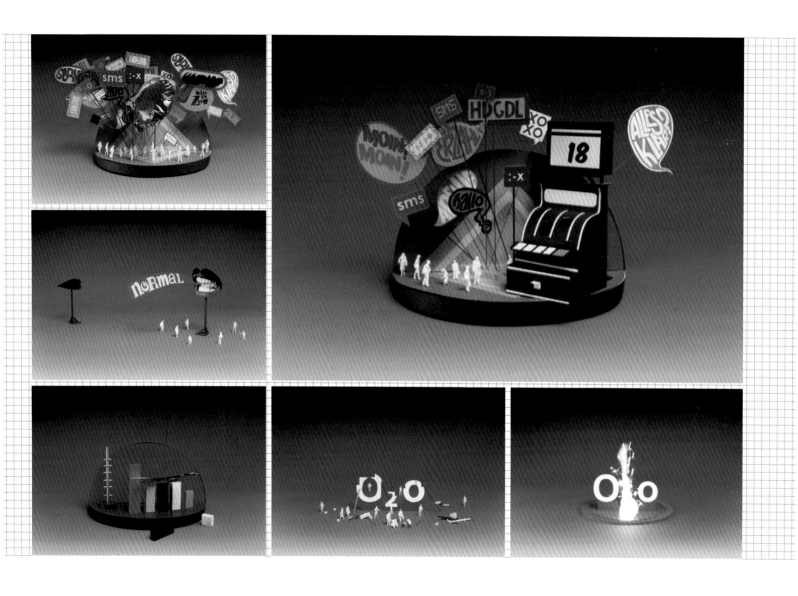

About a year ago, O2 put an end to the tariff "jungle" and set new standards in the market with O2o. The best bit is those who make fewer calls pay less and those who make no calls pay nothing at all! VCCP Berlin came up with an idea of a paper cut story and Parasol Island had the perfect solution. The French director's duo Moustache took out their magic scissors and conjured 83 seconds full of eye candy. Plunge into their lovely miniature world full of paper palms, dinky cars and balloons.

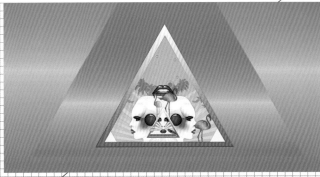

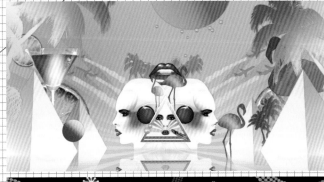

**Project:** Sony Ericsson

**Design Firm:** Parasol Island;
**Animators / Creative Directors:** Steve Scott, Charles Bals, Sebastian Onufszak;
**Motion Designers:** Heike Mauer, Christian Hoffmann, Rupert Mauer, Johannes Albrecht;
**Producers:** Philip Hansen & Viola Habermehl;
**Client:** Sony Ericsson;
**Software:** After Effects, Maya, Illustrator, Photoshop.

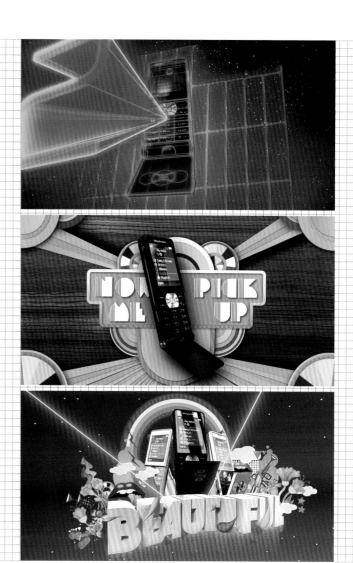

Sometimes a good idea just needs a simple execution, sometimes not. The idea behind this spot is to journey through the music and design styles of the last few decades, like rifling through an extremely cool record collection and pulling out your favorite records. Each of the words of the song will be assigned a particular style responding to a different musical era. Each scene would be transformed from one to the other to create a sense of journey. The final aim is to bring the idea of "listening to your eyes" to life in a contemporary and fresh way.

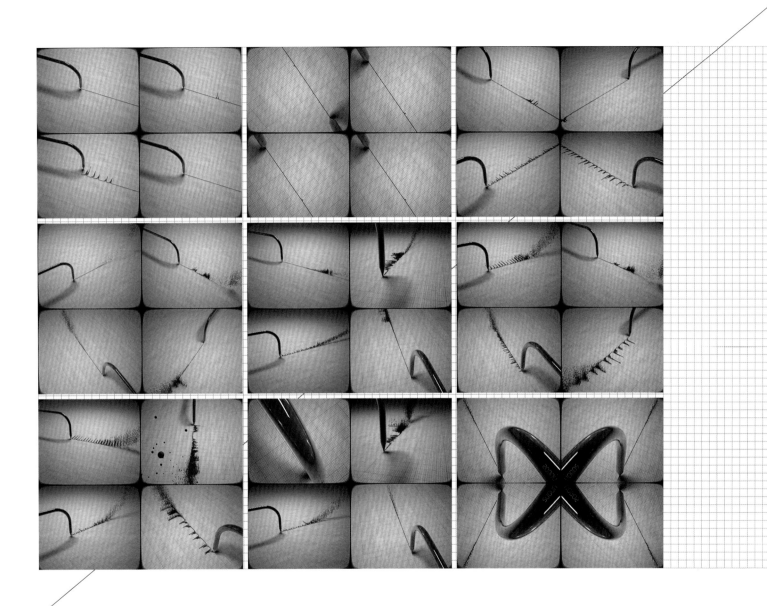

# Project: I'll be Gone

**Design Firm:** KORB;
**Designer:** Rimantas Lukavicius;
**Client:** Mario Basanov & Vidis feat Jazzu;
**Software:** 3ds Max & Adobe Products.

Designed and directed by Rimantas Lukavicius and produced by RGB, this piece of promo was awarded best music video at the Pravda awards in 2008. It was also published in *Digital Arts Magazine* and it is one of the most viewed Lithuanian music videos online.

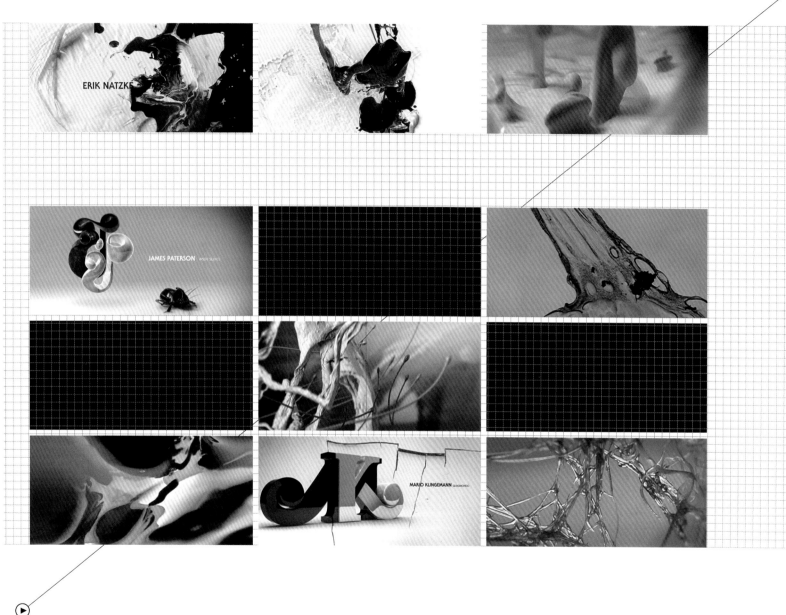

# Project: TOCA ME

**Design Firm:** Dvein;
**Designers:** Fernando Domínguez, Teo Guillem, Carlos Pardo;
**Client:** TOCA ME Design Conference.

Playing with an unusual concept of opening titles and typographic usage, the video is designed to present the creative processes of artists in a metaphorical way. The theme of the video is "Beyond the Surface". The designers represent each artist as a monogram that builds up and the final work came up with a bunch of materials that helps them to put this idea on the screen.

**Project:** Airport

**Design Firm:** TAKCOM;
**Designer:** Takafumi Tsuchiya;
**Client:** Black Sky Recordings LLC.;
**Software:** After Effects .

This short promo is designed by Takafumi Tsuchiya, a director of TAKCOM, and the work is made for Black Sky Recordings LLC. A lot of bokes and lights are used to express the content of lyrics without putting out a definite object.

**Project:** Ida Walked Away

**Design Firm:** TAKCOM;
**Designer:** Takafumi Tsuchiya;
**Client:** Aagoo Records;
**Software:** After Effects.

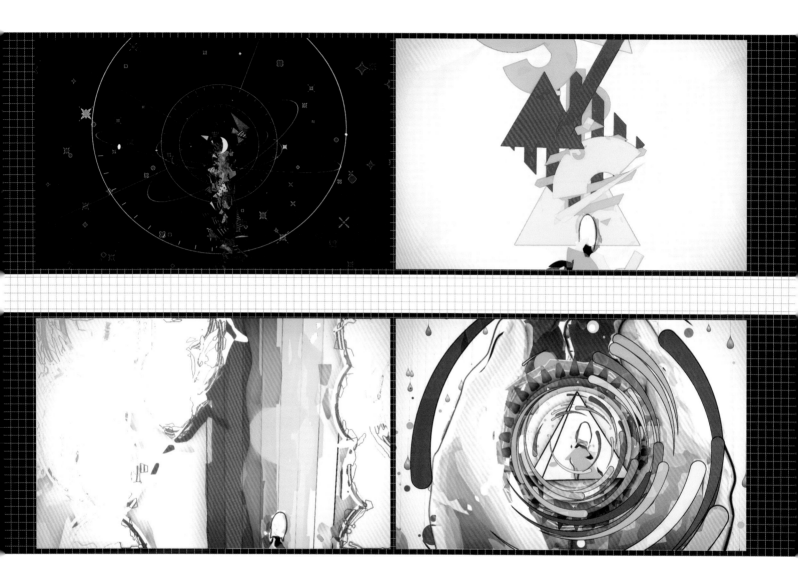

This piece of short promo which is designed and produced by TAKCOM that mixes rotoscoped and animated footage like "take on my style" with the usage of After Effects. All textures come from the shot plate at roadside. The creative work is designed for Aagoo Records.

**Project:** IPhone

**Design Firm:** Materia Blanca – Estudio Visual;
**Designer:** Jeison Barba;
**Software:** Cinema 4D & After Effects.

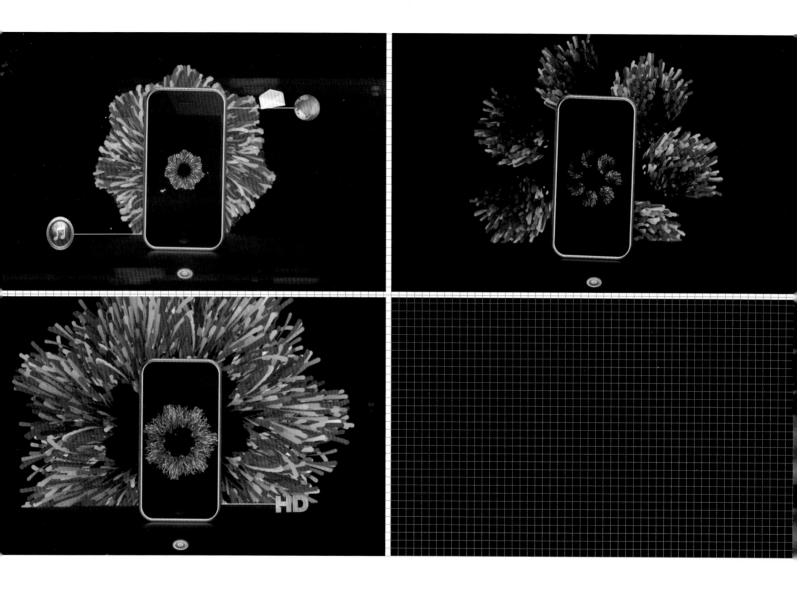

This piece is designed for the presentation of the new Apple IPhone 4, showing its characteristics in an interesting and colorful commercial way. The movement patterns and the contrasting colors create a strong visual effect. This work is prepared as a college's class work without any commercial use.

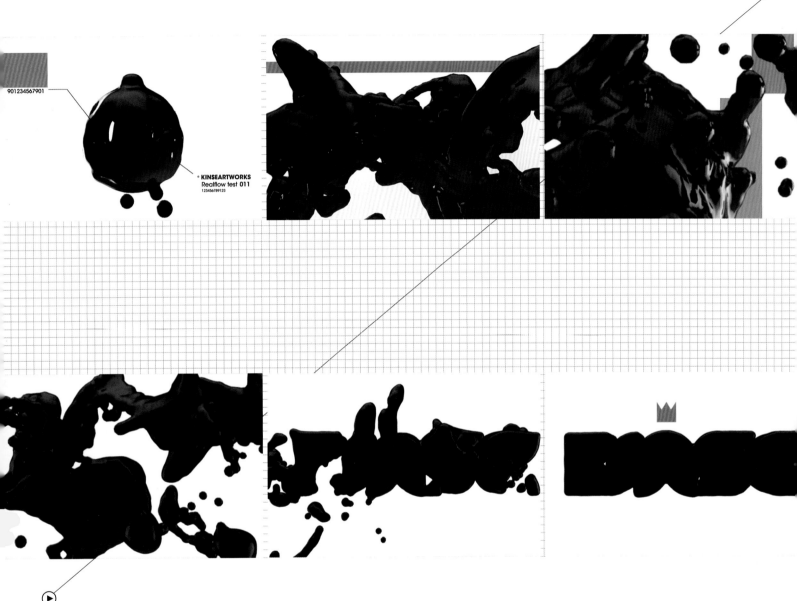

**Project:** Kinse Artworks 2011

**Design Firm:** Kinseartworks;
**Art Direction:** Diego Soto Aguirre;
**Sound Design:** AZ-rotator;
**Client:** Kinseartworks
**Software:** RealFlow, Cinema 4D, After Effects.

Kinse artworks 2011, a self-promotional work, is designed by the motion design team Kinseartworks, and directed by Diego Soto Aguirre. By using the software including RealFlow, Cinema 4D and After Effects, the whole process presents us the Kinseartworks' logotype gradually.

# Project: Madhouse

**Design Firm:** MateriaBlanca – Estudio Visual;
**Designers:** Jeison Barba & Juan Urrego;
**Client:** Madhouse Visual Studio;
**Software:** After Effects, Trapcode Particular V2, Trapcode Straglow 1.6, Optical Flares.

This video is produced to portray Madhouse (Colombian Visual Studios) corporate image. A box contains all the features which identify the company, however, creativity and curiosity are so great that they become impossible to be held in a single box. The result is a colorful and psychedelic explosion.

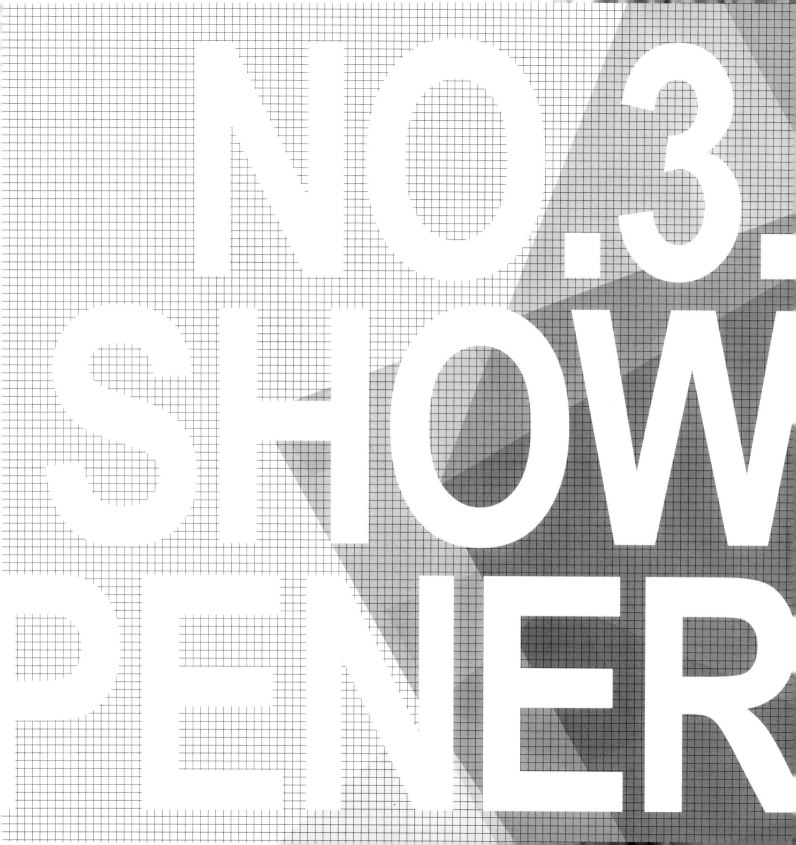

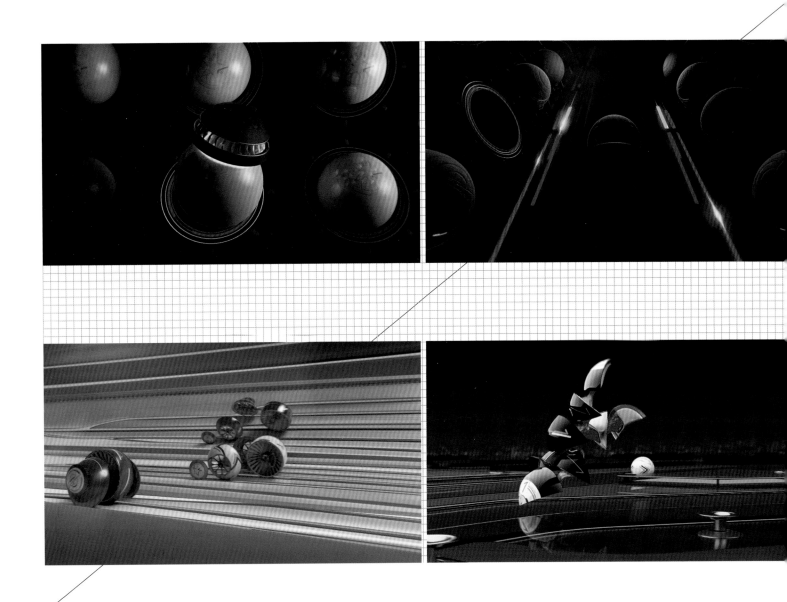

**Project:** MTV European Music Awards Show Ident

**Design Firm:** Dvein;
**Designers:** Fernando Domínguez, Teo Guillem, Carlos Pardo;
**Client:** MTV Europe;
**Software:** After Effects & 3ds Max.

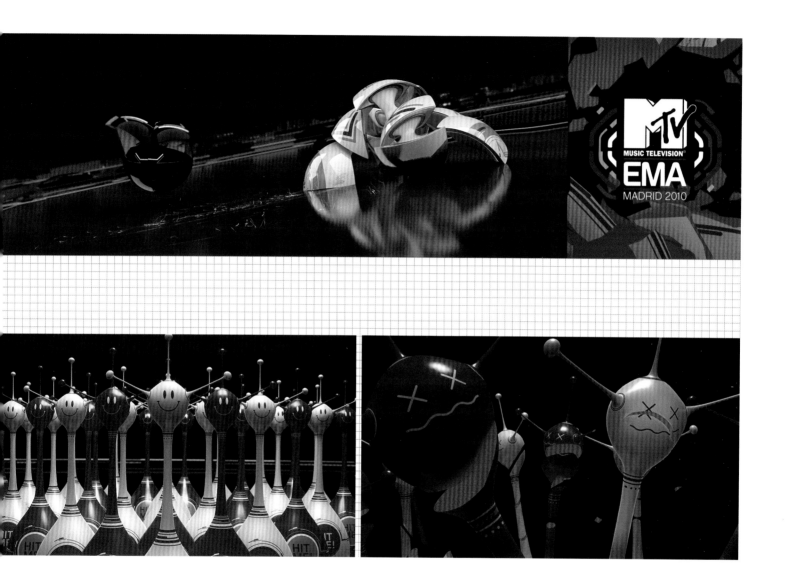

The EMA's show identity is one of the most outstanding musical events of pop music in not only Europe, but all the world. Thus "Impact" is the first word that comes to mind. The designers got the opportunity of adding the fun Dvein spirit to the work to portray the competition with an idea of balls' race, featuring speed, adventure and thrill, which made those concepts visible with a three-dimensional net of slides painted with the vibrant colors from the logo's palette, then made the logo a representation of the competition arena, with several tracks where the balls would compete, and only one can win.

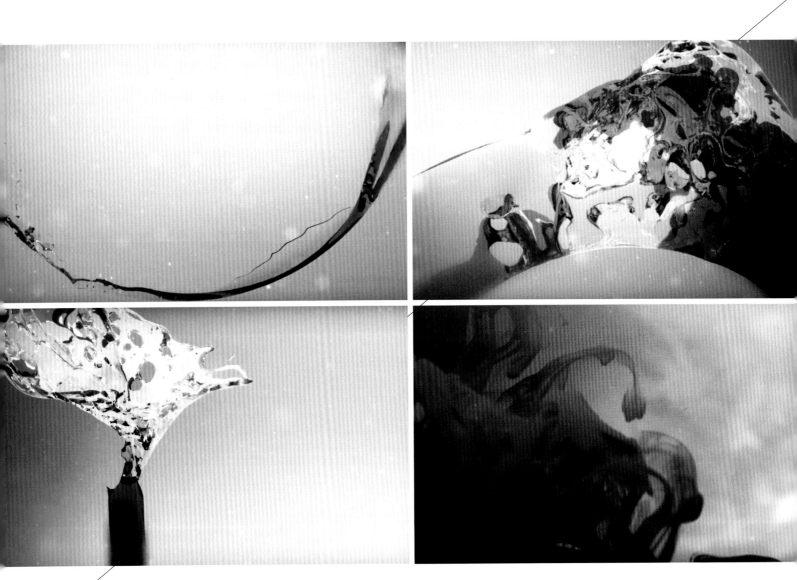

**Project:** Notturno Femminile, Opener TV Show

**Design Firm:** CENTOUNOPERCENTO SRL;
**Art Director / Compositing:** Emiliano Trapani;
**Client:** LA7;
**Software:** 3ds Max, RealFlow, After Effects.

La7 contacted CENTOUNOPERCENTO for the opening sequence of a new TV program which focuses on women and related issues. The idea is to associate the female universe with pure, soft and harmonious images. The staffs designed the logo first, then imported in Max and used it in RealFlow to create the water that generated the letters. To get a warmer feeling, the staffs tinted the letters with ink drops footage. Finally they achieved a more cinematographic look, adding particles and grain, playing with colors, and using a very short depth of field.

**Project:** Weather Update

**Design Firm:** Samaa Creative;
**Designer:** Junaid-Ur-Rehman;
**Client:** Samaa TV;
**Software:** Illustrator, Photoshop, After Effects, Cinema 4D.

This short title sequence is designed for the weather news segment title for Samaa TV. Showing the four seasons in the sequence, the designer, Junaid-Ur-Rehman, adopts several seasonal elements to change over the scenes, like raindrops, clouds, sunny clouds and autumn leaves.

**Project:** Instituto Politécnico ID

**Design Firm:** We Are!;
**Designer:** Rodrigo Miguel Rangel;
**Client:** Instituto Politécnico Nacional (IPN);
**Software:** After Effects, Cinema 4D, Flash, Photoshop.

As a part of the annual promotion of the Instituto Politécnico Nacional (one of the most important educational institutions of Mexico), Rodrigo Miguel Rangel developed this ID which was included in the programming of Once TV Mexico (an educational public television network). Within a seemingly deserted space, all necessary elements to generate new solutions to countless problems were extracted. The use of reflective structures adopting a variety of shapes referred to scientific and technological efforts. The ID was designed in Photoshop, the animation and modeling were created in Cinema 4D, with some elements animated in Flash. The final compositing was done in After Effects.

**Project:** Bing Bang, Promo

**Design Firm:** CENTOUNOPERCENTO SRL;
**Art Director:** Filippo Giacomelli;
**Client:** CARTOON NETWORK;
**Software:** 3ds Max & After Effects.

Cartoon Network Italia contacted CENTOUNOPERCENTO for the promo which mixed the best action cartoons from the channel. The main idea is the explosion, energy explosion. The designers rotoscoped several characters from different cartoons and inserted them in a 3D space where they smashed the cubes in the environment, and made space for the following hero. The promo is very dynamic, young and fresh, and also the music played an important role in achieving such result.

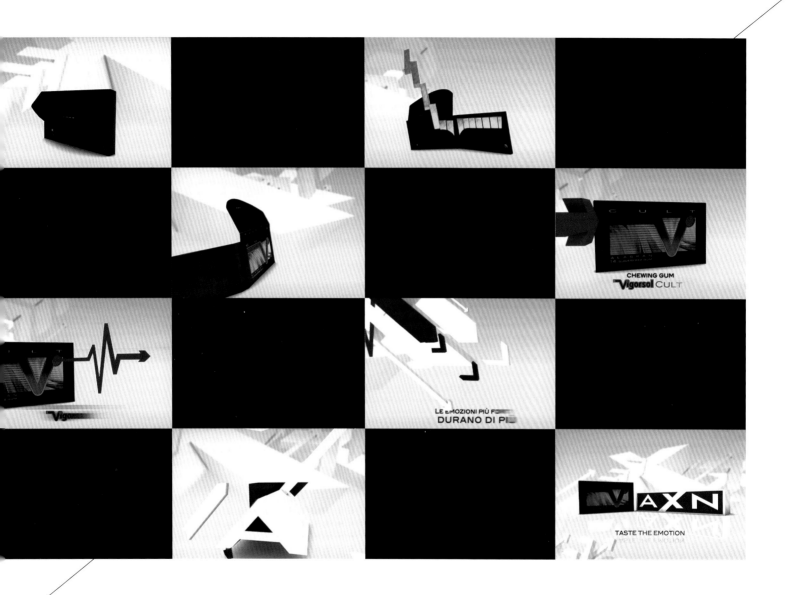

**Project:** Vigorsol AXN, Spot

**Design Firm:** CENTOUNOPERCENTO SRL;
**Designer:** Gabriele Ayache;
**Client:** Forchets;
**Software:** Cinema 4D & After Effects.

Milan-based agency Forchets contacted CENTOUNOPERCENTO for a spot to advertise the new Vigorsol Packaging CULT. The cross promotion between the action TV channel AXN and the Vigorsol brand has to reflect the both brands, so Gabriele Ayache went for something young, fresh and modern: clean background, squared shapes, few strong colors and limited elements. The staffs had the opportunity to freestyle a little bit, which helped a lot to describe the mood of the video well. The arrow, for example, is animated to the beat of music, it changes direction quickly and drive attention from the new Vigorsol packaging to the AXN logo.

# Project: Superstar Series, Opener TV Show

**Design Firm:** CENTOUNOPERCENTO SRL;
**Art Director:** Emiliano Trapani;
**Client:** LA7;
**Software:** 3ds Max & After Effects.

La7 commissioned CENTOUNOPERCENTO for Superstar Series opening sequence which is a very challenging project. The designers shot ink spots themselves and used mattes to link the different 3D shots. They kept the environment quite neutral and focused especially on the cars and the action mood of the video. For the cars, only ambient occlusion and ink & paint were used essentially, and then got a dirty effect on the final composite, adding grain, texture, particles and trails to better emphasize the hard driving style of the car racing.

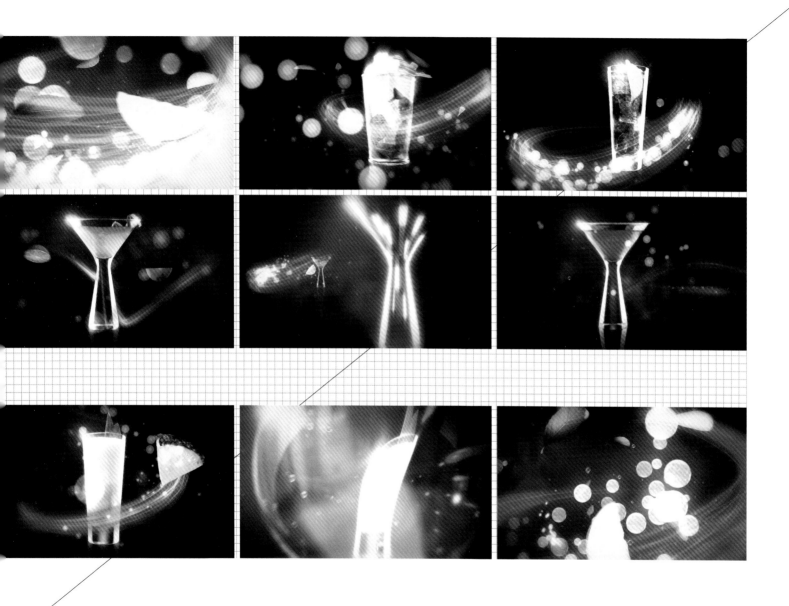

## Project: Bacardi Loop

**Designers:** Carlo Vega & Adam Gault;
**Client:** Bacardi / AgencyNet;
**Software:** After Effects, Photoshop, 3ds Max.

This short promo is designed for Bacardi / AgencyNet, a kind of cocktail. By building smooth, dark and sexy scenes, the designers Carlo Vega and Adam Gault want to show a variety of Bacardi cocktails in the work.

## Project: AXN Bumper Package

**Design Firm:** Jorge Artola Art Direction & Motion;
**Designer:** Jorge Artola;
**Client:** AXN Spain;
**Software:** Cinema 4D, After Effects, Final Cut Studio 3.

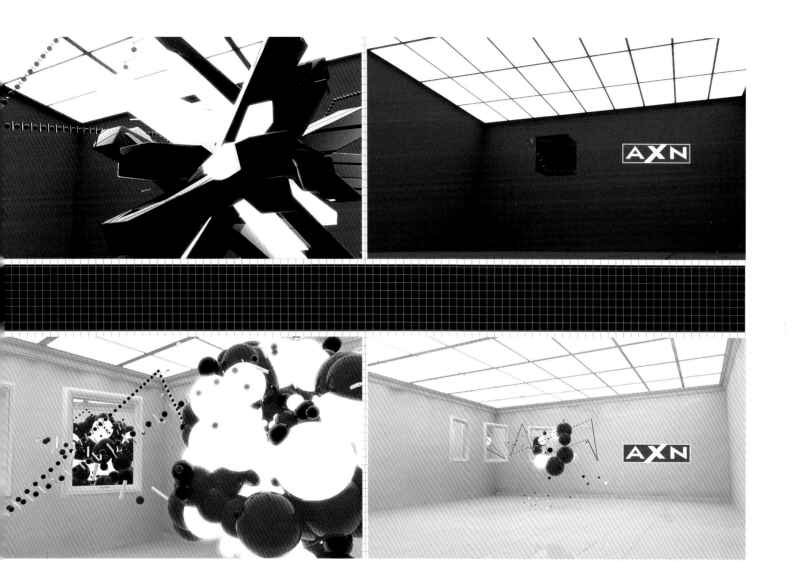

This Bumper Package proposal is designed for AXN Spain by the design team of Jorge Artola. The goal is to show the 3 main genres of the channel's TV shows in a new and fresh way: Action, Drama & Thriller, and represent them in single 4-second pieces.

## Project: BUSKUL – Intro Sequence

**Design Firm:** Phosworks Digital Industries;
**Designer:** Jonas Strandberg Ringh;
**Client:** SVT;
**Software:** After Effects & Photoshop.

This is an intro sequence designed for the critically acclaimed Swedish children's television show "BUSKUL". The motion design studio Phosworks Digital Industries takes charge of the whole design process. As a chief designer, Jonas Strandberg Ringh adopts old photos, painting board and other elements to annotate the work.

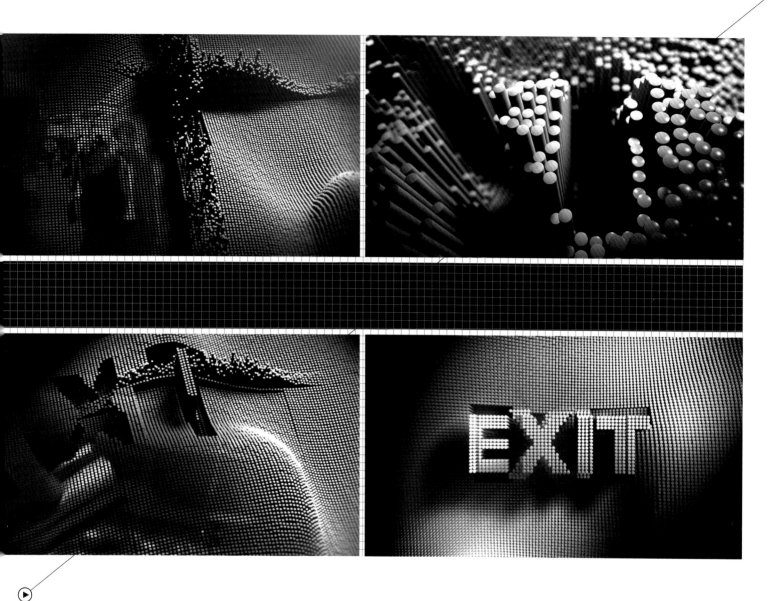

## Project: Exit, Opener TV Show

**Design Firm:** CENTOUNOPERCENTO SRL;
**Director:** Fabio Calvi;
**Art Director / Compositing:** Emiliano Trapani;
**Client:** LA7;
**Software:** 3ds Max & After Effects.

La7 commissioned CENTOUNOPERCENTO for re-branding of the TV political programme "EXIT". Being a program focuses also on journalism, with several guests that debate on current issues, the design team decided to use the pin box image as a concept that reflects the different public opinions, people, issues, point of views of our time. Most of the animation is done in Autodesk Max where the single pins are drive-animated by grey maps. The final composite is done in After Effects where lights, colors, depth of field and also some images are added.

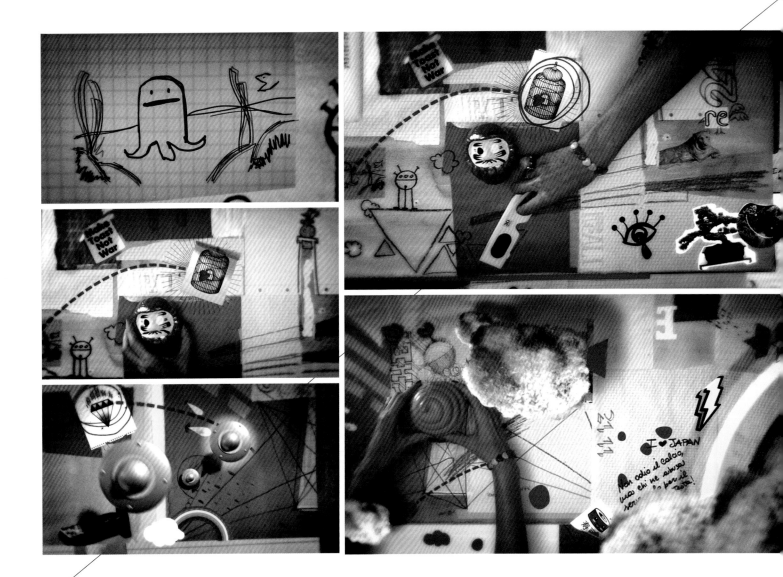

**Project:** Vite Reali, Opener TV Show

**Design Firm:** CENTOUNOPERCENTO SRL;
**Art Director / 2D Animation:** Emiliano Trapani;
**Client:** RAI4;
**Software:** After Effects & Maya.

Vite Reali is a talk show that focuses on web celebrities and everything that regards the net. There's a guest who is invited to describe and illustrate internet contents and curiosities. CENTOUNOPERCENTO studio produced the opener sequence: the basic idea is to reflect the spirit of the program as a flying over the mixture of the web. The staffs shot the actor in their studio and composed it with miscellaneous objects, cut-outs and sketches in After Effects. The balloon at the end is made in 3D, and it works as a key transition to the program.

## Project: Mochilao MTV Brazil

**Design Firm:** ONIX – Motion Stuff;
**Creative Directon:** Ralph Karam – Le Cube;
**Art Direction:** 2Veinte;
**Animation:** Leonardo Rica – ONIX;
**Client:** Ralph Karam – Le Cube for MTV Brazil;
**Software:** After Effects, Cinema 4D, Photoshop.

The main idea of this project is to create a world that could represent the feelings and tastes of a backpacker's world mixing different animation styles. This world is made entirely in Cinema 4D, trying to make 3D polygon-made style environment which get completed with a traditional 2D animation for the ocean and waves. Finally, an After Effects finishing is made for the compositing, color correction, lights and details. The concept of the moving camera is used to place the viewer in a first personal travel through this unique MTV world.

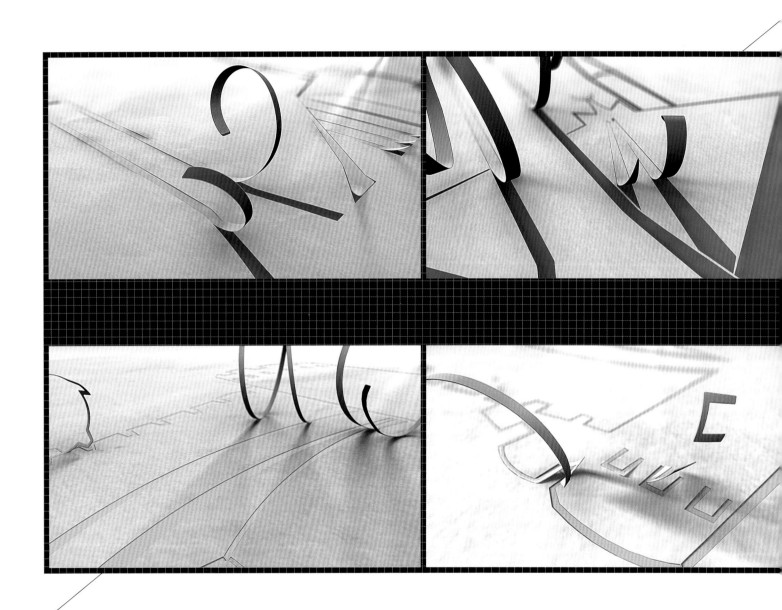

# Project: Regional Idents

**Design Firm:** CNBC Creative;
**Designer:** Junaid-Ur-Rehman;
**Client:** CNBC Pakistan;
**Software:** Illustrator, Cinema 4D, Photoshop, After Effects.

To meet the request of CNBC Pakistan, Junaid-Ur-Rehman is asked to make a series of idents shows which present different regions of Pakistan. To reach this goal, the designer visited and photographed many famous monuments in the big city, and created this series of promos finally.

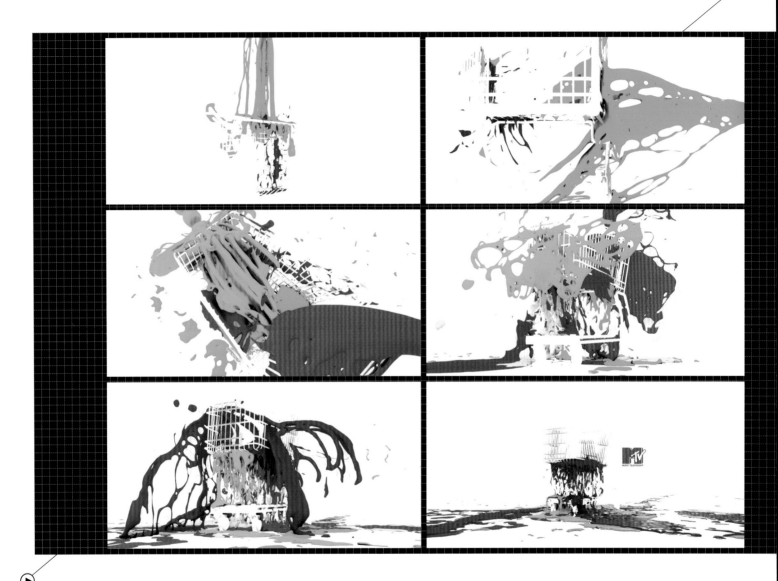

**Project:** Swatch MTV Playground's 10th on MTV Competition

**Design Firm:** Binalogue;
**Concept / Director / Design:** David Carrizales;
**3D:** David Carrizales & Alvaro Martín;
**Motion Graphics:** David Carrizales;
**Music:** Claudio Bonaldi 'Noise Colors';
**Software:** After Effects, RealFlow, 3ds Max, Maya.

This is the entry for the Swatch MTV Playground's 10th on MTV Competition which is conceptualized, directed, designed and developed by Binalogue. The competition brief is: "What would you do with 10 seconds of on-air time for MTV?" David Carrizales played an important role in the whole design process and this piece of promo won the first prize.

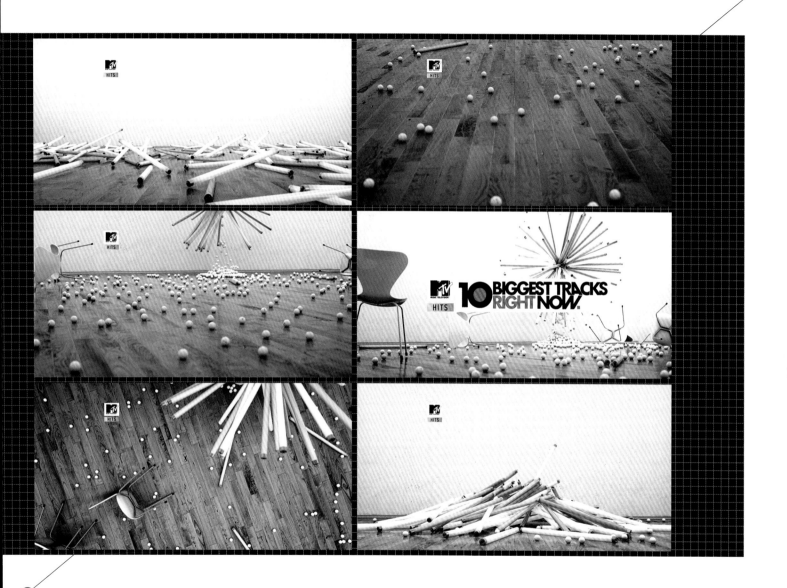

**Project:** MTV Hits – 10 Biggest Tracks Right Now

**Design Firm:** KORB;
**Designer:** Rimantas Lukavicius;
**Creative:** Sven Muller;
**Client:** MTV Networks Australia;
**Software:** 3ds Max & Adobe Products.

Designed by KORB studio, this show packaging is a part of MTV Hits packaging visual music. It is an open brief with only one rule which is pink color. This is a director's cut version which is not the final version on air. And it can be seen mostly in Australia and various online blogs.

**Project:** ATV – The Business of Love

**Design Firm:** EAT MY DEAR;
**Designers:** Markus Hornof, Patrick Sturm, Simon Griesser;
**Client:** ATV;
**Software:** Cinema 4D, After Effects, Illustrator, Photoshop.

Doing broadcast design is always nice, especially when you have a lot of freedom to make a case for ATV, a private broadcast channel in Austria. For the new show "The business of love", EAT MY DEAR developed the complete TV package including show logo, opener animations, bumpers, etc. Referring to the show's title, they came up with the idea to find themes (like money, love, etc) related to the content and finally found a symbol that would transport all those characteristics, the Matrjoschka.

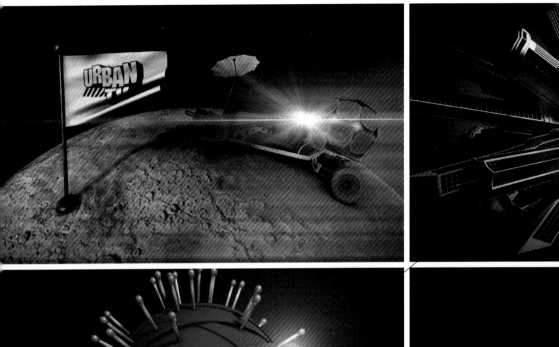

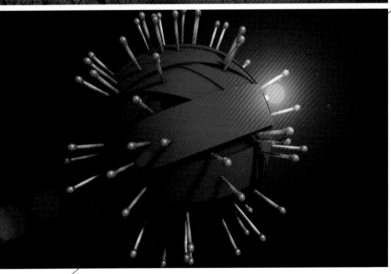

**Project:** Urban TV

**Design Firm:** EAT MY DEAR;
**Designers:** Markus Hornof, Patrick Sturm, Simon Griesser, Isabella Thaler;
**Production Company:** PostPanic;
**Client:** Universal Music Media;
**Software:** Cinema 4D, After Effects, Illustrator, Photoshop.

Universal Music commissioned EAT MY DEAR to create a presentation movie for their Music TV Channel "Urban TV". The movie showcased the different program formats along with the channel's identity, all in an unique and not too serious way but always related to the content of each format. Their design approach is to work with just one centered object, which could showcase the different formats of the channel by transforming into content-related visual metaphors reaching from urban music to gossip, to classic, to backstage, to rated ... To get a one-flow clip, the team also connected the separate formats and made transitions as seamless as possible.

I WANT MY MTV

N DO
AN NG

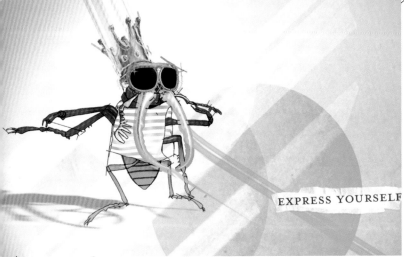

EXPRESS YOURSELF

MEN,
WE BELIEVE
THE POWER OF YOUT

**Project:** MTV – This is Our Brand Story

**Design Firm:** EAT MY DEAR;
**Designers:** Markus Hornof, Patrick Sturm, Simon Griesser;
**Production Company:** PostPanic;
**Client:** MTV Netherlands;
**Software:** Cinema 4D, After Effects, Maya, Illustrator, Photoshop.

WE INSPIRE YOUTH
CHANGE THE WORLD

When the design team Eat My dear started working on the concept for this brand movie, they already had some key statements of MTV. From there they developed a story by creating motives and mental bridges for all the statements. They bypassed too obvious visual solutions in reflecting the statements, so they decided to use a strong imagery which could tell a story on its own. One major challenge was to accomplish everything on their wish list within the deadline, as the team wanted a visually rich piece at the end. They also had to keep in mind that the single parts had to be connected to each other, so they had to plan their animations properly to make transitions as smooth as possible.

## Project: Agri Business

**Design Firm:** CNBC Creative;
**Designer:** Junaid-Ur-Rehman;
**Client:** CNBC Pakistan;
**Software:** Illustrator, Photoshop, After Effects, Cinema 4D.

This short promo, Agri business, is a show opener designed for CNBC Pakistan. The show is about the agricultural business and trends, so in the sequence, the designer Junaid-Ur-Rehman showed all four major crops – wheat, cotton, rice and sugar cane – which have been grown in Pakistan.

**Project:** Volaris TV Graphics Package

**Design Firm:** Binalogue;
**Client:** Volaris;
**Concept / Director:** David Carrizales;
**Design:** David Carrizales & Sergio Tomasa;
**3D:** Sergio Tomasa;
**Motion Graphics:** David Carrizales & Sergio Tomasa;
**Software:** After Effects & XSI.

This TV graphics package is conceptualized, directed and developed by the design team Binalogue. It is designed for the in-flight entertainment channel of Mexican Airline Volaris. The application of bright colors indeed adds some lively feel to the passenger without any doubt.

## Project: ChillOut (TV Show Opening Titles)

**Design Firm:** Sounas Design;
**Designer:** Ilias Sounas;
**Client:** ChillOut;
**Software:** After Effects, Illustrator, Flash.

It is an animated video with opening titles and bumpers for the ChillOut TV show. The show is a TV Magazine with various topics such as lifestyle, cooking, nightlife, interviews and fashion, etc. The client wants a minimal but fresh approach for the opening video, so the viewers can easily identify the show's genre. The video contains mainly simple shapes in vivid colors, which are choreographed based on the show's music theme.

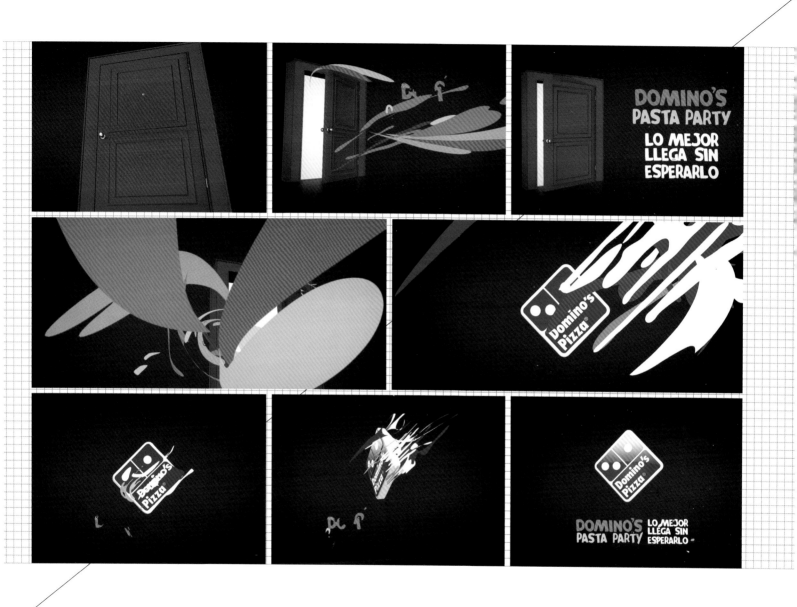

## Project: Domino's Pasta Party

**Design Firm:** MVS Televisión;
**Designer:** Kike del Mar;
**Client:** Domino's;
**Software:** Cinema 4D, After Effects, Photoshop, Illustrator.

This short promo is made for the opening of a spot called "Domino's Pasta Party". Kike del Mar and his design team, MVS Televisión, are in charge of designing this project. It is about the new products of Domino, showing how people can win a party sponsored by Domino.

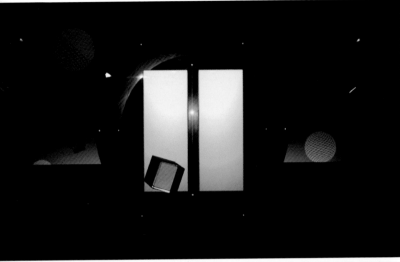

**Project:** Pausa

**Design Firm:** MVS Televisión;
**Designer:** Alfredo Villa;
**Client:** MVS Televisión;
**Software:** Cinema 4D, After Effects, Photoshop, Illustrator.

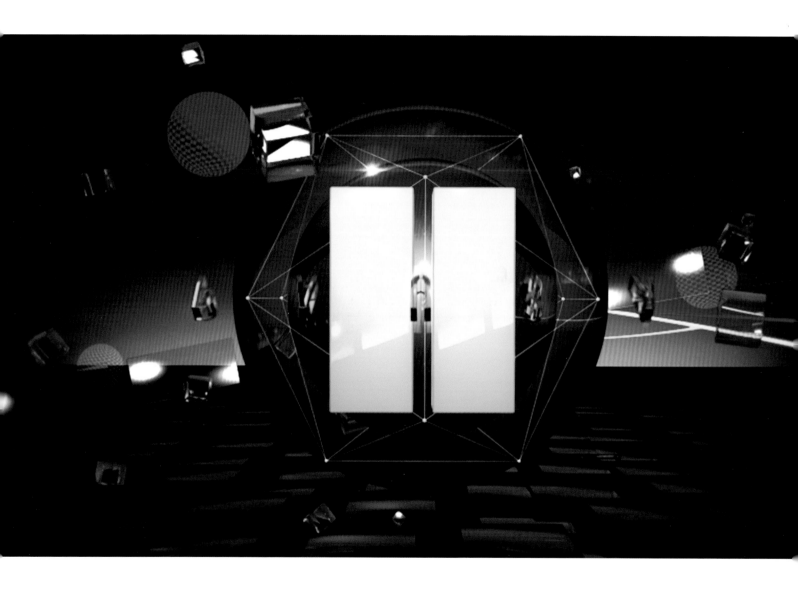

This project is made for a Music TV Show in MVS Televisión, showing the top ten of a week. The company needs a graphic package for this bloc of programming. For the opening, they want something very geometric, with 3D basic objects and shiny textures, something like the boss says "basic". And this is the final result, and the TV show is still on the air.

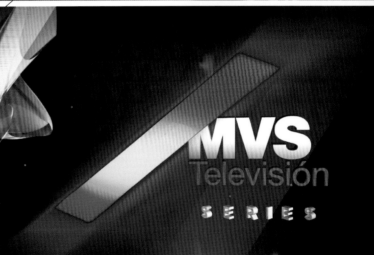

**Project:** Series Originals

**Design Firm:** MVS Televisión;
**Designer:** Alfredo Villa;
**Client:** MVS Televisión;
**Software:** Cinema 4D, After Effects, Photoshop, Illustrator.

The project is designed for the opening of the TV show's bar in MVS Televisión. Each show, including this opening, was made in house before starting. This is just for emphasizing the productions made by the same company. They wanted an image with the rainbow colors like the inclined line that is part of the MVS logo. So the designers used this range of colors to make the entire opening, and for the end, they used the institutional logo of the company.

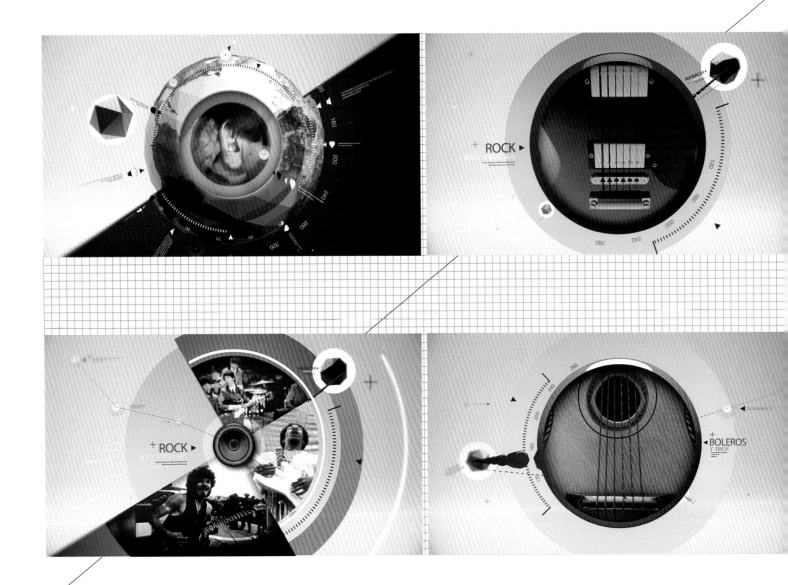

**Project:** Conexiones Teaser

**Design Firm:** MVS Televisión, Motion Graphics Area;
**Designer:** Pavel Molina Rivera;
**Client:** MVS Televisón;
**Software:** Cinema 4D, After Effects, Photoshop, Illustrator.

Conexiones (Connections) is a television show that tries to show all the different types of music around the world and how they are connected in time and space by unknown and curious events in an indirect way. In the teaser, the concept is represented with molecules. Each molecule contains a music gender, and inside of it are images of the most representative artists of different decades. While the teaser goes on, all the connections are uncovered as well as the huge amount of musical genders and the connection between them. Everything starts and ends in the same place, with the TV show's logo. This creates a never-ending cycle and definite connection between all the musical and visual concepts of the show, as well as the constant use of circular forms as a visual representation of this infinite repetition cycle.

**Project:** 13 Edición Festival de Málaga de Cine Español 2010

**Design Firm:** EMedialab & Whiteline Studio;
**Designer:** Pablo Olmos Arrayales;
**Client:** Festival de Málaga de Cine Español;
**Software:** 3ds Max & After Effects.

The Málaga Spanish Film Festival (FMCE) has been running annually since 1998 in Malaga, Spain. In this event, the most relevant Spanish feature film releases are presented, awarding the best films of the year. Based on the design of the Festival ident clip on the Festival logo and award: a biznaga (a typical flower from Málaga), the proposal of this piece of motion design does not reveal the logo from the beginning, and the designers got it using very close shots. The viewer just can see drops of white paint that creates a structure. When the biznaga is completely built, it freezes and bursts from inside like a shower of colors making up the 2010 edition poster.

**Project:** MTV Casi Mas

**Design Firm:** MTV Design Services Latam;
**Creative Director / Director:** Camilo Barría;
**Designers:** Camilo Barría & Matías Fernández;
**Audio:** Marco Camacho;
**Client:** MTV Networks Latinamerica;
**Software:** After Effects & 3ds Max.

Created by the team MTV Design Services Latam, this title sequence is made for MTV Networks Latinamerica. Lights shine momentarily without departing from the mass, but make strange sculptures to remain in time. The application of bulbs makes the whole design unique and creative.

**Project:** 10 Most

**Design Firm:** Muz-tv Design Department;
**Designer:** Sergey Rybkin;
**Client:** Muz-tv;
**Software:** After Effects, Photoshop, 3ds Max.

The project titled "10 most" is designed by Sergey Rybkin. It is a promo of the customer TV channel of Muz TV which is located in Russia. The customer TV channel is a popular broadcast that plays once a week. It has a new theme each time, such as 10 greatest busts, 10 most noisy rock musicians, and so on.

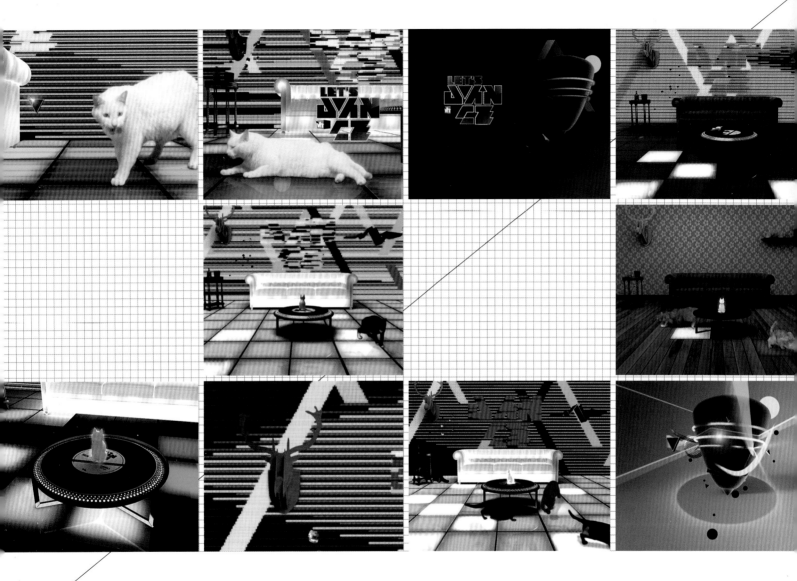

# Project: Let's Dance

**Design Firm:** Jalea.tv;
**Designers:** Jalea.tv + Jose Jimenez (r3nder.net), Mauro Petrelli (3D environment);
**Client:** MTV Networks Latin America;
**Software:** Illustrator, After Effects, Photoshop, 3ds Max, Cinema 4D.

Pre-dancing hour, an empty house, cats, LED screens, etc., anything is possible to be used. Following the idea of the pre-dancing hours, the designers of Jalea.tv imagine an empty house where the cats take over and turn everything upside down. All the furniture responds to the music, and the house becomes a disco party inspired by Billy Jean!

# Project: Ritmo da Folia

**Design Firm:** Jalea.tv;
**Designers:** Jalea.tv, Mariano Armengol, Catriel Martinez;
**Client:** Lifestyle TV Brazil;
**Software:** Illustrator, After Effects, Photoshop.

The Brazilian Carnival is held as a celebration of women, color and rhythm. And the task of making promos is handed over to the motion design team Jalea.tv. To portray these elements, the designers adopt bright color and bold, abstract eyes designed to give a vivid description of this carnival.

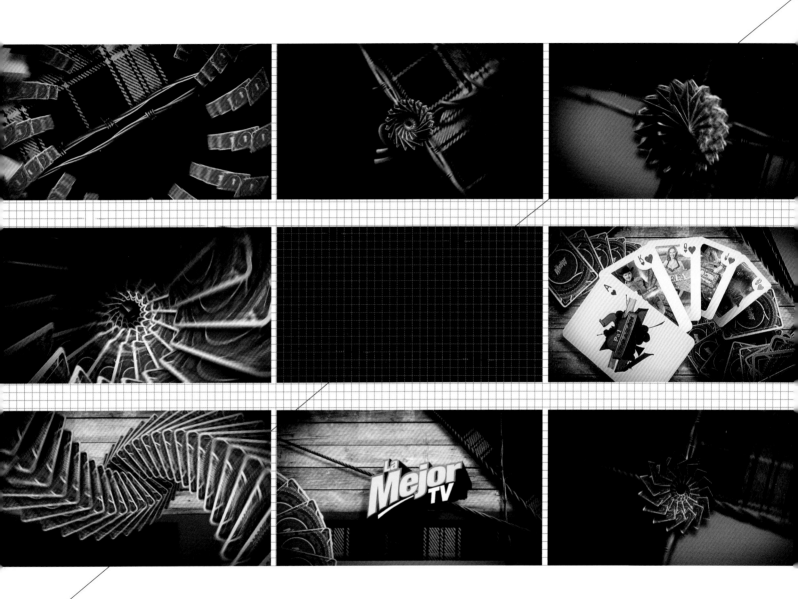

**Project:** La Mejor TV Channel Promo

**Design Firm:** MVS Televisión;
**Designer:** ROAN;
**Client:** MVS Televisión;
**Software:** Cinema 4D, After Effects, Photoshop.

As the chief designer for this short channel identifications, ROAN designed it for a Mexican TV channel. It is for their weekly TV show, a program which is based on the idea of gambling cards and betting that they've got the best poker in hand.

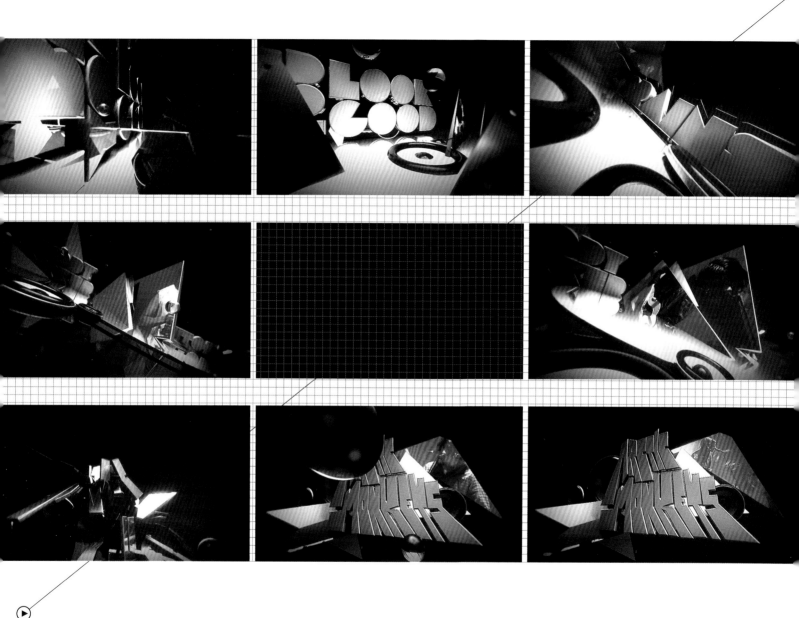

**Project:** Arctic Monkeys Live in Mexico

**Design Firm:** MVS Televisión;
**Designer:** ROAN;
**Client:** MVS Televisión;
**Software:** Cinema 4D & After Effects.

Arctic Monkeys Live in Mexico is a TV opener served for a special program, which is about the Arctic Monkey's concert offered in Mexico City in 2010. Adopting profound colors such as purple and mandarin blue makes the scene refined and fantastic.

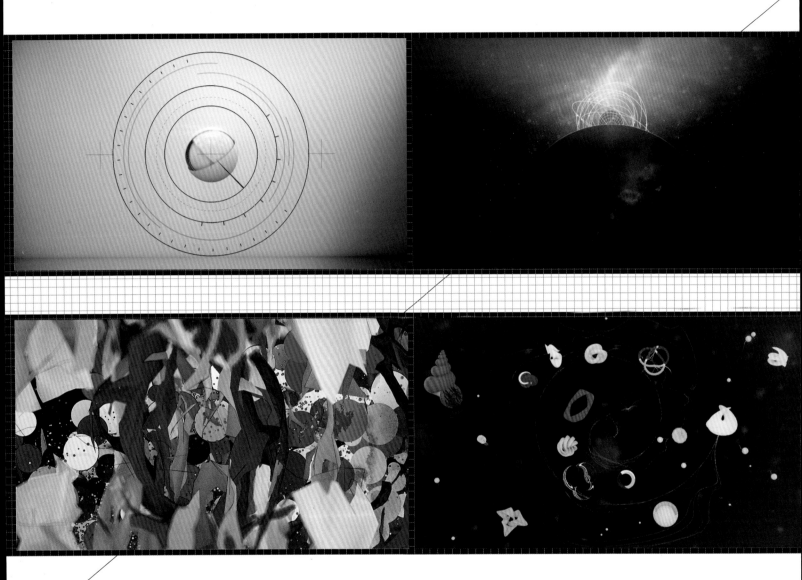

**Project:** Space is the Place

**Design Firm:** TAKCOM;
**Designer:** Takafumi Tsuchiya;
**Client:** Space shower TV INC;
**Software:** Cinema 4D & After Effects .

"Space is the Place" is a station ID which is designed for a music broadcasting channel in Japan. The designer, Takafumi Tsuchiya, adopts various external elements and characters of the television satellite to be connected and presented in the short promo.

**Project:** La Mejor TV Channel

**Design Firm:** MVS Televisión;
**Designers:** ROAN & Kike del Mar;
**Client:** MVS Televisión;
**Software:** Cinema 4D, After Effects, Photoshop.

This piece of short channel identifications is designed for a Mexican TV channel based on all the variety of the norteño music genre which is popular in the Mexican culture and southern United States as well. ROAN and Kike del Mar from MVS Televisión work on this project together.

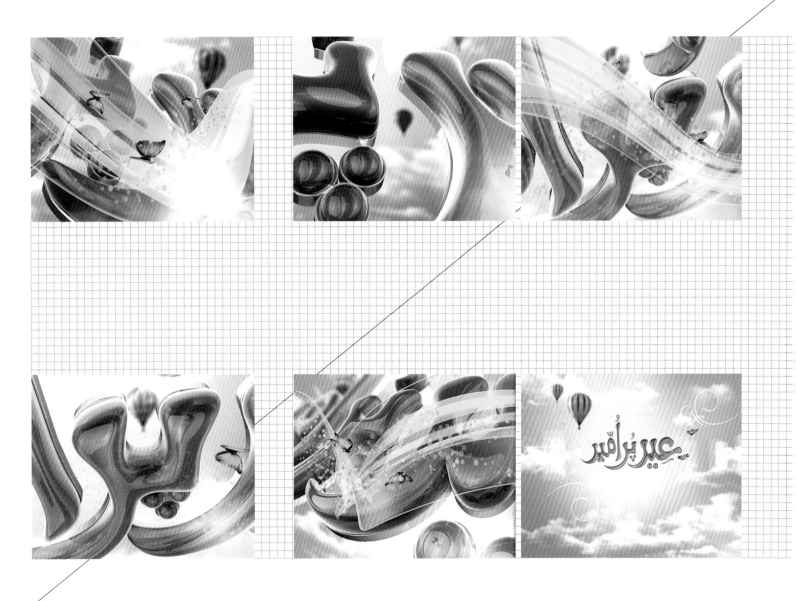

# Project: Eid-Ul-Fitar Ident

**Design Firm:** Dunya News Creative;
**Designers:** Syed Ijtaba & Junaid-Ur-Rehman;
**Client:** Dunya News;
**Software:** Cinema 4D, Illustrator, Photoshop, After Effects.

The short film is designed for Eid which is a traditional festival that Muslims celebrate after the holy month of Ramadan. The ident shows joy and happiness via the expression of bright colors and vivid scenes. The words which come up in the end (Eid Pur Umeed) mean hopeful Eid.

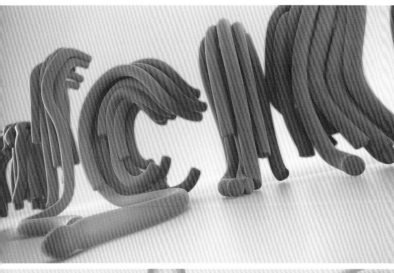

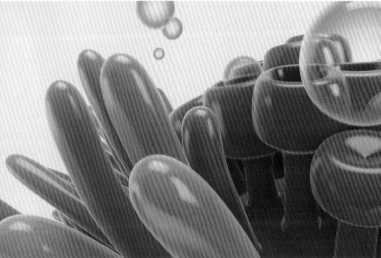
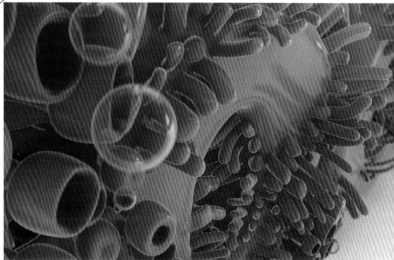

**Project:** Nickelodeon HD

**Design Firm:** ManvsMachine;
**Designers:** Mike Alderson, Tim Swift;
**Animation:** Remi Dessinges, Shane Griffin, Simon Holmedal, Rupert Burton, Richard Thomas;
**Client:** Nickelodeon's HD Channel;
**Software:** Adobe CS, Maya.

ManvsMachine won a competitive pitch to direct & animate a series of logo idents for Nickelodeon's HD channel. The brief was to create an evolution of Nickelodeon's "one-brand" to show-off the networks recently added high-def capabilities. The response was this investigation of form and texture, with one foot in the real world and the other in a slightly strange child's imagination.

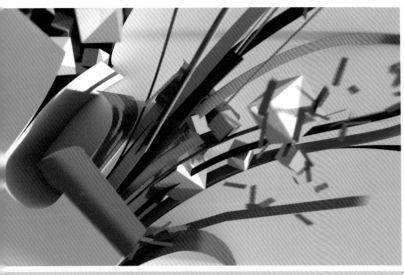

## Project: Syfy

**Design Firm:** ManvsMachine;
**Designers:** Mike Alderson, Tim Swift;
**Sound Design:** Rich Martin;
**Client:** Sci Fi Channel of Syfy;
**Software:** Adobe CS, Maya.

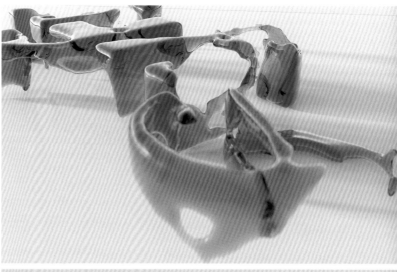

In July 2009 the Sci Fi channel relaunched as Syfy. ManvsMachine joined forces with fellow London design studio Proud to collaborate from the pitch stage of the rebrand project, tasked with designing and releasing the new on-air look. The brief asked for an own-able and distinguishable solution, retaining the positive associations from the genre of science fiction, whilst appealing to a broader audience and embracing the benefits of imagination.

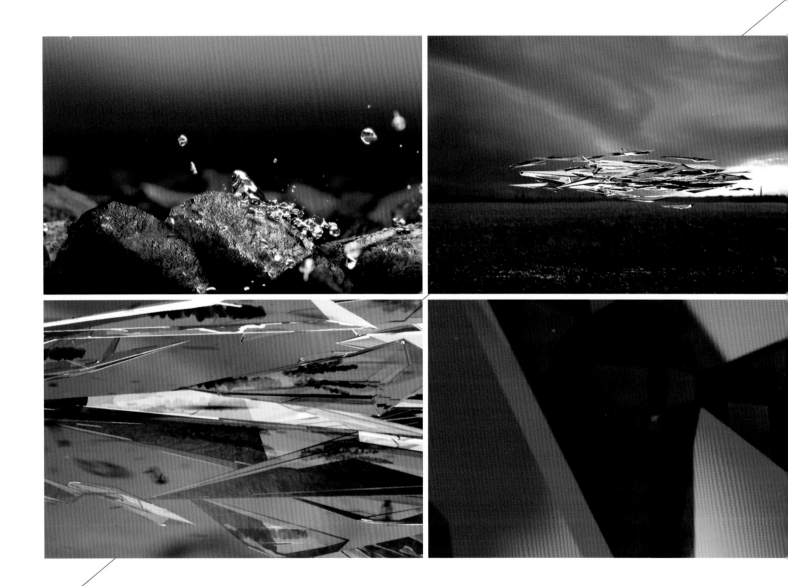

**Project:** Field

**Design Firm:** Selfburning;
**Designer:** Nick Luchkiv;
**Software**: After Effects, 3ds Max, RealFlow.

The video "Field" is a short film showing the transformation and morphing of a strange object setting against a rural scene of Russian countryside. Polyangular objects try to recover their native form. It plays around with the concept of field, from the sense of farming land to an electric field.

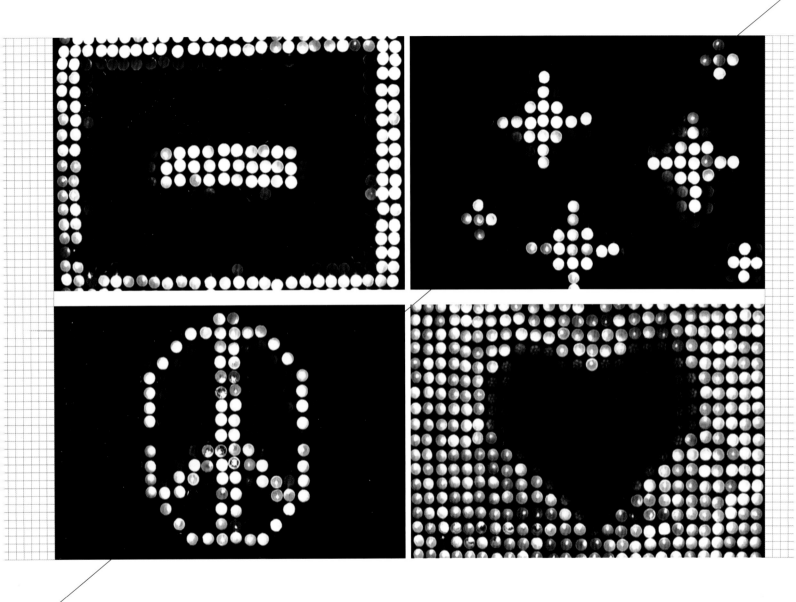

**Project:** VH1 Holiday Card / Candle Stop Motion

**Design Firm:** VH1 In-House Design;
**Designers:** Julie Ruiz, Jimmy Wentz, Jonathan Cooper;
**Client:** VH1;
**Software:** After Effects.

Every year, the in-house design team VH1 is asked to create a VH1 holiday card for all the employees to be able to send out. And this year, they did a lot of brainstorming and came up with the idea of creating a stop-motion movie using candles. With a very minimal budget they purchased a bunch of tea light candles, lighters and a 6-pack of beer, with the video camera fixed to the end of a broom and attached the broom to a ladder. After editing and bringing in the music and story line, it all came together, and it really proved that you don't need a huge budget to do something really creative and special.

**Project:** Esoteric Mash Up

**Designer:** Cento Lodigiani;
**Client:** Self-promotion;
**Software:** After Effects.

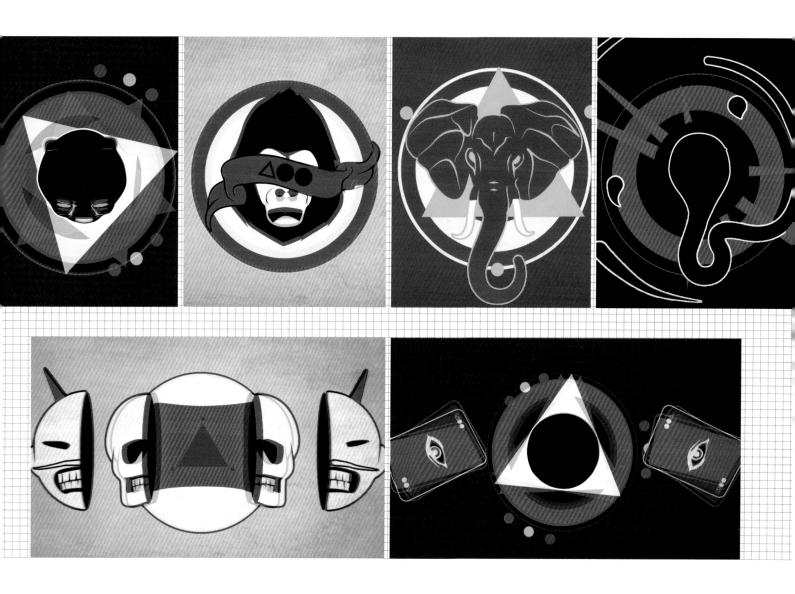

It's a hypnotic and intense music-driven flow of faces and icons, like the result of some esoteric vision or nightmare. The animation has been fully made in After Effects using masks and puppet tools to interpolate the shapes. Just one plug-in has been used to create the RGB timewarp effect.

**Project:** Morning Walk

**Designer:** Cento Lodigiani;
**Client:** Self-promotion;
**Software:** After Effects.

This motion design is a digital art experiment in 2D animation, aiming to promote the Cento Lodigiani brand. Some silly colorful characters walking in a row does not seem to give too much importance to the strange behavior of their heads. They simply follow their goal: walk walk walk! And never look back. Everything has been created in Adobe After Effects with the use of animated masks and puppet tools. Some specific animations have been created frame by frame like the characters walk cycle.

**Project:** Animation Tag Attack Episode 8

**Designer:** Scott Benson;
**Client:** Animation Tag Attack;
**Software:** After Effects, Photoshop, Flash, Sound Forge.

Animation Tag Attack is an international "exquisite corpse" style project involving some fantastic animators using different styles and ideas to continue the story. Each participant gets 4 weeks to produce between 5 and xx seconds of film. When the time is up, the clip gets uploaded to the blog and the next one in line takes over. It is up to each individual creator to pick the style and media they want to work in – and to decide how they think the story should evolve.

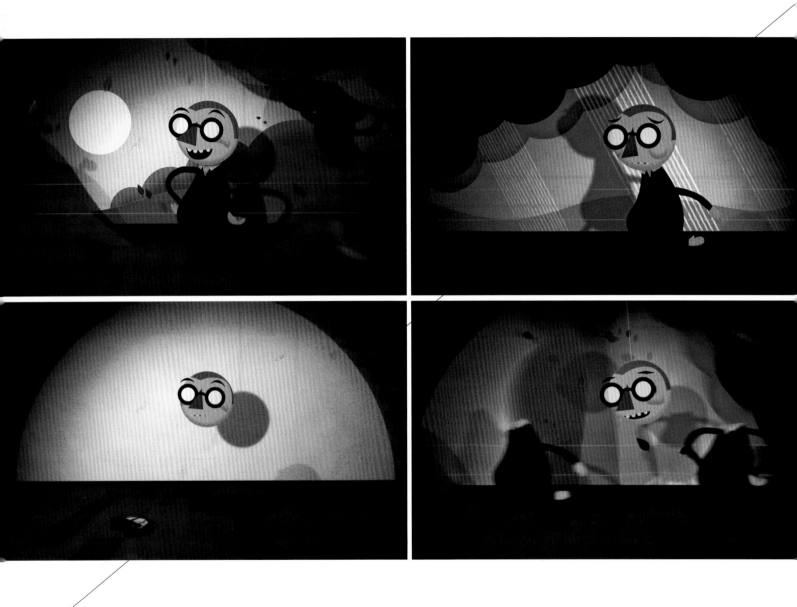

**Project:** On the Subject of Depression

**Designer:** Scott Benson;
**Client:** Self-promotion;
**Software:** After Effects, Photoshop, Sound Forge.

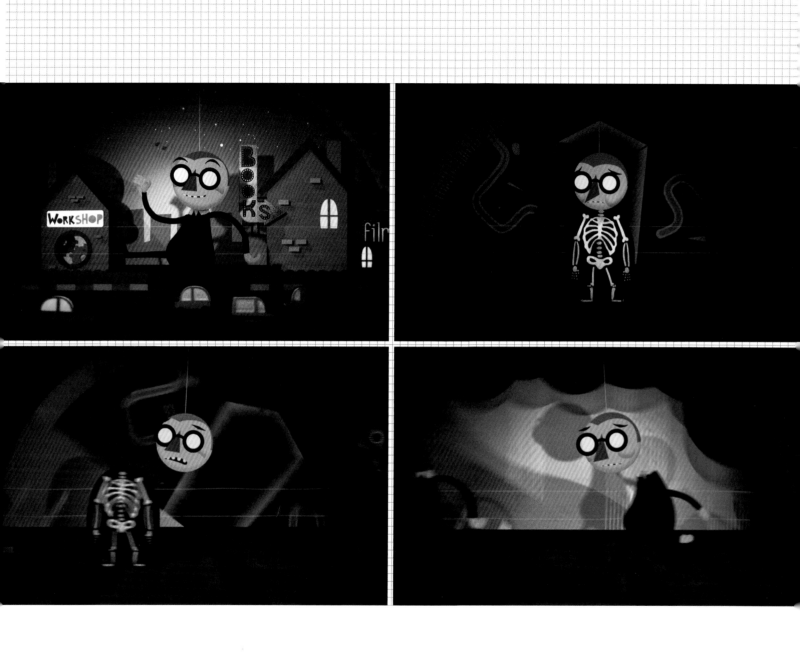

Scott Benson suffered from a mild form of depression. He made this work hoping it would be a comfort to others who might have similar issues. It certainly helped him to talk openly about it, and Scott received many wonderful emails from other people who struggle with the same issues. This project reminded you that as an artist, your greatest tool in dealing with issues like this is your own creativity. Sometimes the act of creating something is enough to give you the strength you need.

**Project:** Rebranding

**Designer:** Scott Benson;
**Client:** Self-promotion;
**Software:** After Effects.

# SEGRE GATION
**DIFFERENT PEOPLE.**  **DIFFERENT PLACES.**

WHAT ARE YOU MAKING?
WHAT ARE YOU DESIGNING?
WHAT ARE YOU BRANDING?
**WHAT ARE YOU ADVERTISING?**
WHAT ARE YOU REBRANDING?
WHAT ARE YOU GREENWASHING?
WHAT ARE YOU PROMOTING?

As creative people, designers are often called upon to lend their talents and skills to give a new face to a product, a company, or a questionable idea. The designer holds the belief that segregation is terrible – morally, socially, philosophically and historically. To show how easily – through cute, approachable, creative advertising – something truly horrifying can be rebranded, repackaged and promoted.

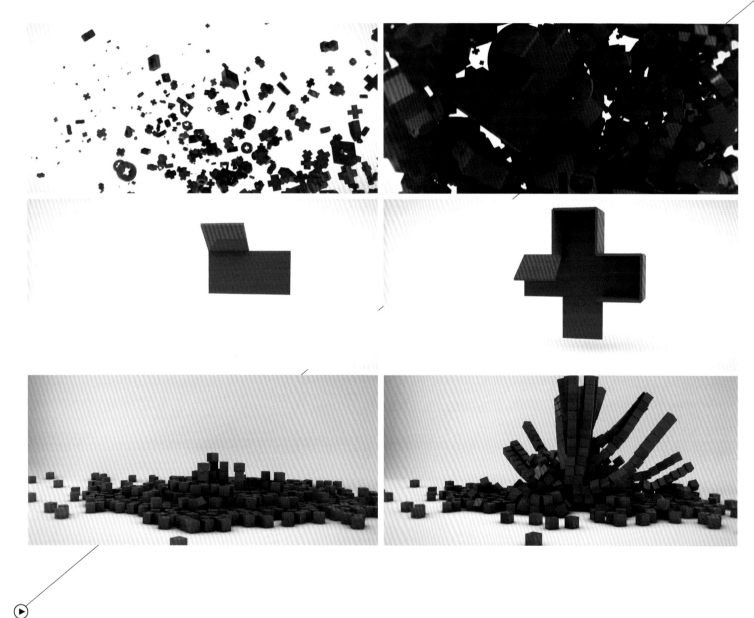

**Project:** Swiss Inspiration

**Design Firm:** Zapum.org;
**Designer:** Zapum;
**Software:** Cinema 4D, After Effects, Premiere.

Ein ausländer in der Schweiz

This series of teasers were made during a stay in Switzerland with the intention of developing skills in Cinema 4D and After Effects in free time. But the result proved to be much more interesting, and turns out to be a unique piece of motion design.

**Project:** StarWars vs. StarTrek

**Design Firm:** Lichtfaktor;
**Designers:** Marcel Panne, David Lüpschen, Tim Fehske;
**Client:** Sky Movies (UK);
**Software:** Premiere.

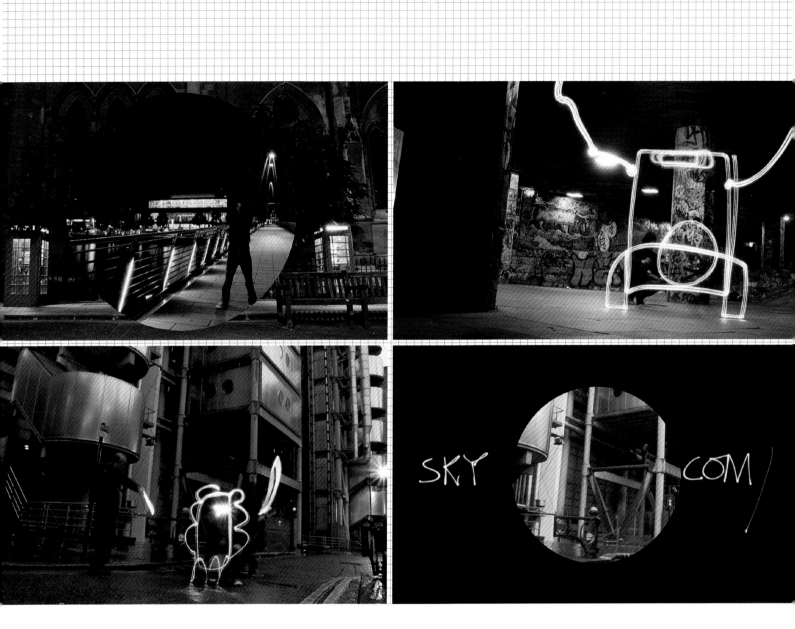

StarWars vs. StarTrek is shot in London during 4 days and the completed video is done spontaneously. It becomes the tipping point of the career of Lichtfaktor and of the international lightwriting trend. It has more than 1 million clicks in less than a month and many new jobs and festival invitations worldwide.

**Project:** Talk Talk

**Design Firm:** Blinkink;
**Light Artist:** Lichtfaktor.
**Client:** Talk Talk;
**Software:** After Effects;

Shot in South Africa, Talk Talk is designed by Noah Harris of Blink Ink. It takes 3 days to complete the work with some talented people's help, such as Dayton Taylor from "Digital Air", Hector Macleod from "Glassworks", Toby Howell who created many outstanding works including "The Fantastic Mr. Fox" and "Shaun the Sheep" and, last but not least, the mighty Noah Harris.

**Project:** Lovely Day

**Design Firm:** Mica;
**Directors / Designers:** Luca & Sinem;
**Software:** Maya, After Effects, Photoshop.

Mica wants to prepare an animated Valentine's card for Valentines Day, flavoring with odd characters and an ironic approach. The designers aim to build a loving short film via the interesting expressions of scenes and characters which are designed in Maya, After Effects and Photoshop.

**Project:** Mica Promo

**Design Firm:** Mica;
**Directors / Designers:** Luca & Sinem;
**Software:** Maya, After Effects, Photoshop.

This 40-second short film is a self-promotional work designed to launch the new animation studio of Mica. In the film, a colorful giant snail and a girl crash with the Turkish villager who is driving and takes him to the fantasy world of Mica.

**Project:** HU-KANTEE-HAN

**Design Firm:** Marblart;
**Designer:** Maarten Berkers;
**Client:** Boomoperators;
**Software:** Final Cut, After Effects, Photoshop, TV-paint.

HU-KANTEE-HANG is the title of the track that Maarten Berkers animated for Dutch hip-hop formation Boom operators. This video is his graduation project at the School of Visual Arts Utrecht. The lyrics spit by MC Rescue are used as a guide to visualize the video. The audio of Kid Sundance is energetic and rough, which is expressed visually by using a hasty paste, limited colors, strong contrasts and dirty backgrounds. Maarten tries to make a sleek rollercoaster ride which feels like a camera movement switched between live-action shots and animation on paper. He films the artists and two poodles in front of a green screen and draws 1500 animation frames manually on A3 paper with ink and brushes, and then scans them into the computer.

# Project: Transform

**Design Firm:** Konacoast;
**Designers:** Jasper Hesseling, Maarten Berkers, Rob Klunder, Joost Penninx;
**Client:** Elsevier;
**Software:** Final Cut, After Effects, Photoshop, TV-paint.

The design concept of the Transform video is based on KAPLA, small wooden construction planks that are used as kids toys. By adding the simple white lines, the designers visualize a helper who helps the builder to gain his goal. By using these simple expressions, the 2D lines and 3D animated KAPLA planks come together well. The final video is clean and easy to understand.

# Project: Primitive Love

**Design Firm:** DI-T;
**Designer:** Dimo Trifonov;
**Software:** After Effects & Cinema 4D.

Dimo Trifonov wants to capture this primitive act of love in just a few seconds. What he wants to express in the short movie is the feeling that even the simplest object can look more primitive. Even though the frames seem to be simple, the constant changes add bright spots to the whole design.

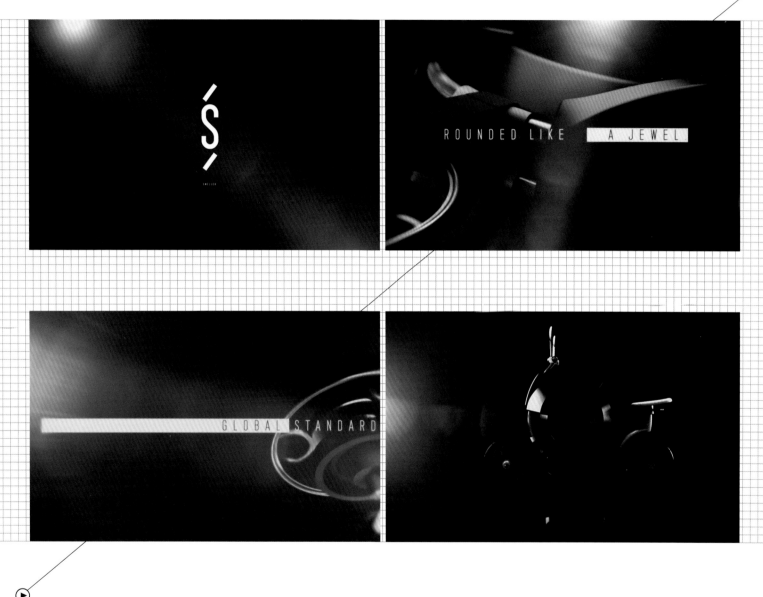

## Project: Sweller

**Design Firm:** Maxilla inc;
**Designer:** Ryunosuke Shimura;
**Client:** Hiroshi Sudo;
**Software:** After Effects, Premiere, Cinema 4D.

This is a conceptual motion design work for "Sweller". The concept of "Sweller" is smooth, elegant and hype. This work is not for commercial use, and only aims at research by using some software including After Effects, Premiere, and Cinema 4D.

## Project: Receptorium

**Design Firm:** Ar2 Studio;
**Designer:** Artur Jurzyk;
**Client:** Microkino.pl;
**Software:** After Effects, Premiere.

This video is designed for promoting a non-profit cultural project "Receptorium" which is held in Warsaw, Poland. The mentioned event takes place in an old abandoned cinema where children are watching ecranisations of obligatory school readings. The show is organized by VJ collective Microkino.

**Project:** Prisma Forest – Prisma Sky

**Design Firm:** Sulfurica Motion Design;
**Designers:** Claudio Guerra, Freddy Guerra, José Fernández;
**Client:** Prisma TV;
**Software:** After Effects, 3ds Max, Final Cut Studio.

The purpose of this project is to create break bumpers for a Chilean Graphic Design TV Show called Prisma. Prisma is broadcasted on the international signal of TVN (Televisión Nacional de Chile). In this project, the design team is free to create anything they want, so they come up with the idea of creating a surreal world in which magic is enhanced with vivid colors, and the power of music achieves this through the mix of different techniques.

**Project:** Beta Boardshop

**Design Firm:** Sulfurica Motion Design;
**Designers:** Claudio Guerra, Freddy Guerra, José Fernández;
**Client:** Beta Boardshop;
**Software:** After Effects, 3ds Max, Final Cut Studio.

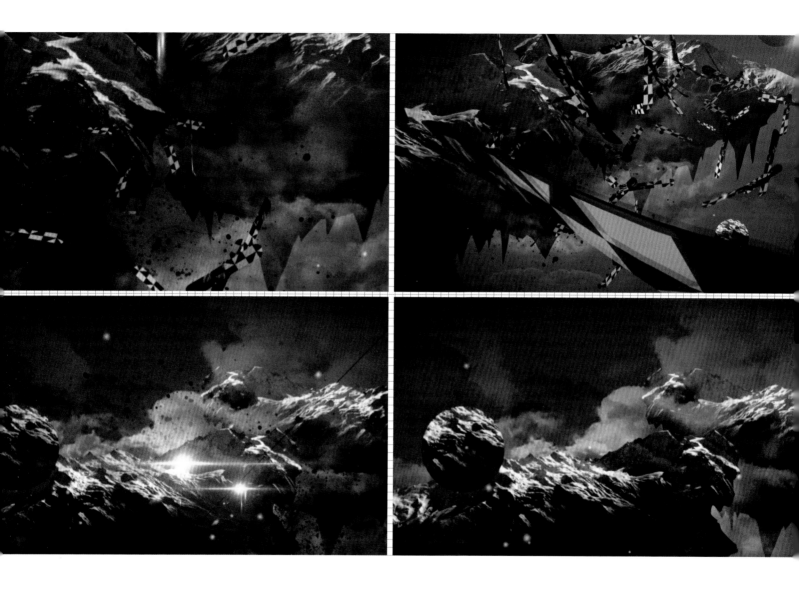

Sulfurica Motion Design is asked by friends from Beta Boardshop to develop an unique piece of television advertisement for the 2010 winter season. This has no limitations with the topic of the artwork, so it allows the imagination to work freely and with no attachments. In this animation, the designers want to take the snowboard out from typical space and bring it to another galaxy in which they spread like a plague.

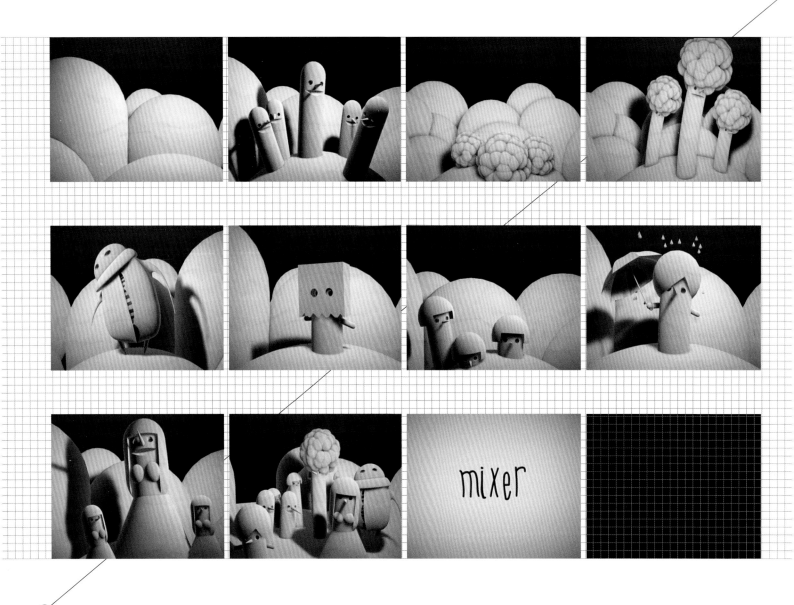

**Project:** Mr. Sandman

**Design Firm:** Mad.tv in-house;
**Designer:** Chaidalis Constantinos;
**Client:** Mad.tv;
**Software:** After Effects & Cinema 4D;

The TV show intro designed for Mad.tv. Mr. Sandman is a personal project that goes on air. In fact, the designer recounts that at the time he was working on something else, so while After Effects was rendering he was playing on Cinema 4D with very basic shapes. The original idea is to make a video with musician-look-alike sausages.

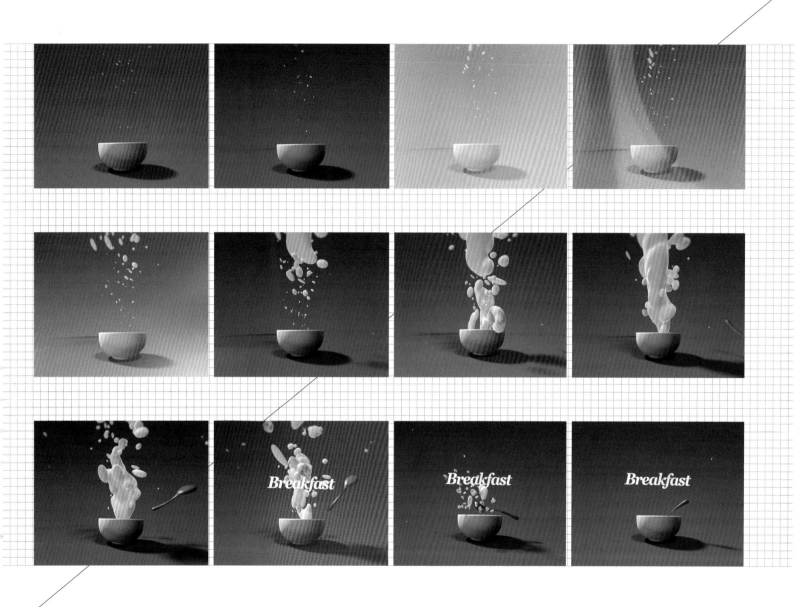

## Project: Breakfast

**Design Firm:** Mad.tv in-house;
**Designer:** Chaidalis Constantinos;
**Client:** Mad.tv;
**Software:** After Effects & Cinema 4D;

This is a TV show intro designed for Mad.tv. The concept apparently is the classic breakfast Corn Flakes in an explosive slow motion animation. The client wants it time-remapped and more faster, so the designer Chaidalis Constantinos makes some speed adjustments.

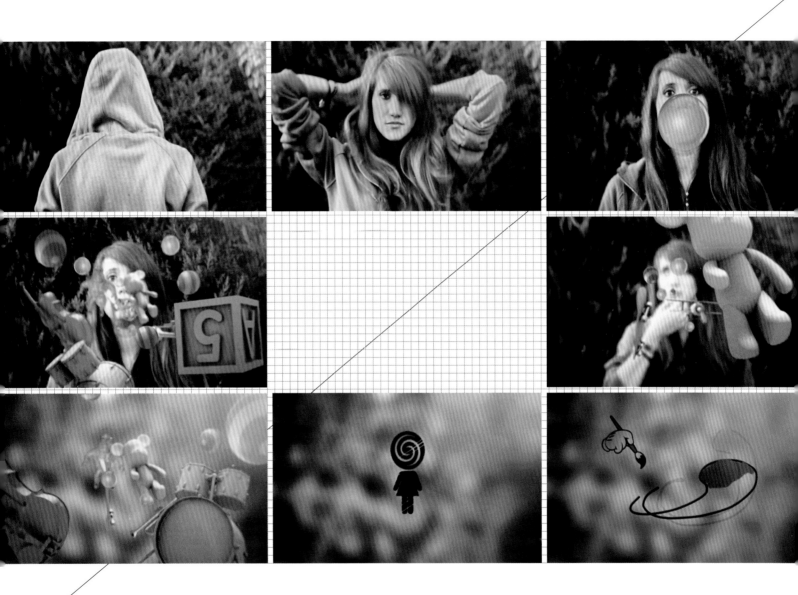

**Project:** Funked

**Design Firm:** Mad.tv in-house;
**Designer:** Chaidalis Constantinos;
**Client:** Mad.tv;
**Software:** After Effects & Cinema 4D;

"Funked" is one of the most hilarious show on Greek TV. The designer Chaidalis Constantinos started working on the project by shooting the footage of the show's hostess. After the shooting which is outdoors, the staffs made some color correcting and compositing.

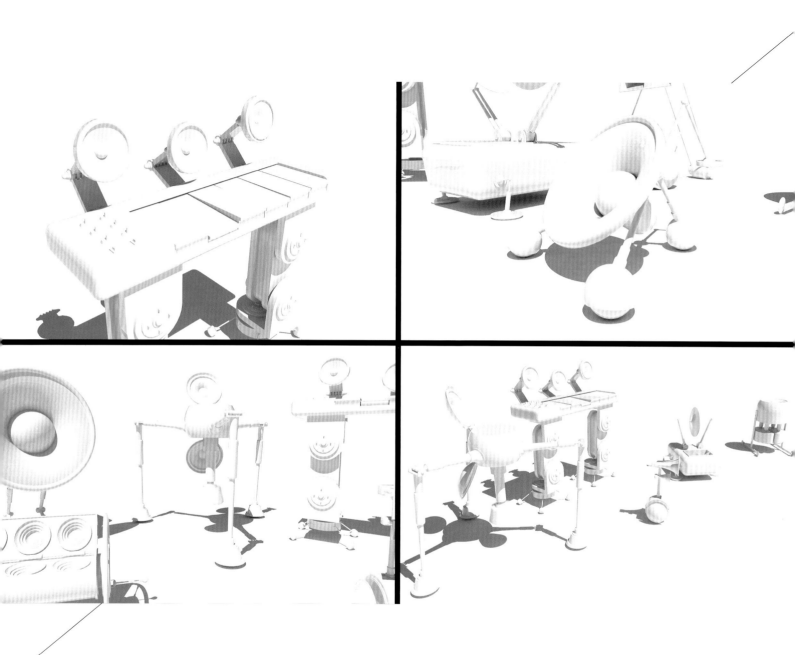

# Project: I Am a Robot I Love Music

**Design Firm:** Zapum.org;
**Designer:** Zapum;
**Software:** 3ds Max, After Effects, Premiere.

Unimate's 8373 is automatically controlled, reprogrammable and designed to play electromechanical beats. Any robots of this series can interact with each other, and the result is powerful music.

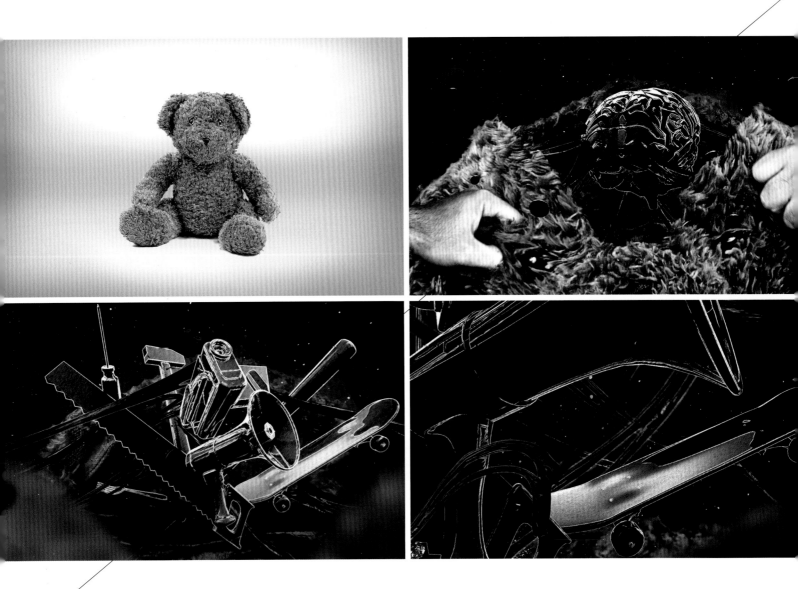

**Project:** Dudes of Hazard

**Design Firm:** Drool Studio;
**Designers:** Jorge Artola, Fernando Navarro, Edu Martinéz;
**Client:** Zoopy TV;
**Software:** Illustrator, Photoshop, After Effects, Premiere, Cinema 4D.

Drool Studio is invited to work with Zoopy TV on the Re-brand & Idents Package for their newest reality show called "Dudes of Hazard". For the intro they focus on the "funny" thing, the main aspect of the show, as an evolution from something "cute" to something "rude".

**Project:** 8tv Channel Ident (Freakout Friday)

**Design Firm:** Motiofixo;
**Designers:** Shah Azman, Ajwad Ajinda, Izuin Zulsyamin;
**Client:** 8tv;
**Software:** After Effects, Photoshop, Illustrator .

The design team's concept is making the work as freaky as they can by the expression of transforming humans to cartoon monsters. In the video, the crowd of crazy running people freak out, and then suddenly transform into monsters. These amazing sequences add some interesting effects to the whole design.

**Project:** MTV Hits

**Design Firm:** Mirari & Co;
**Director:** Jimmy Yuan;
**Client:** MTV AUS;
**Software:** 3ds Max, Final Render Stage 1, After Effects.

The idea is to transform fun, coolness of the music into abstract art forms. The video starts off with a postmodern abstract object resembling a pair of speakers moving rapidly synchronized to the beats of the track. The object is constantly expanding, contracting and changing as if it's the emitter of the sound track sending out sound waves. As the music tempo gets faster, the composition launches a network of visual elements interacting to the track and expanding into infinity. In order to make the music as the core of the work, a technique is used to link music waveforms to the abstract object. So the movements of the object are driven by the sound.

**Project:** MTV – Weekend Guide

**Design Firm:** Anti;
**Animation:** Animasjons Departementet;
**Art Direction:** Kjetil Wold & Martin Yang Stousland;
**Project Manager:** Tine Moe;
**Client:** MTV;

MTV Weekend Guide is a weekly show on MTV showcasing the events that take place next weekend. This stop-motion analogue show is put together by hours of paperwork, cutting pieces of paper and then reverting it all. This is what happens if you are already tired of your night out and start dreaming of what the posters of next week will showcase! This piece is used for MTV Nordic and Japan!

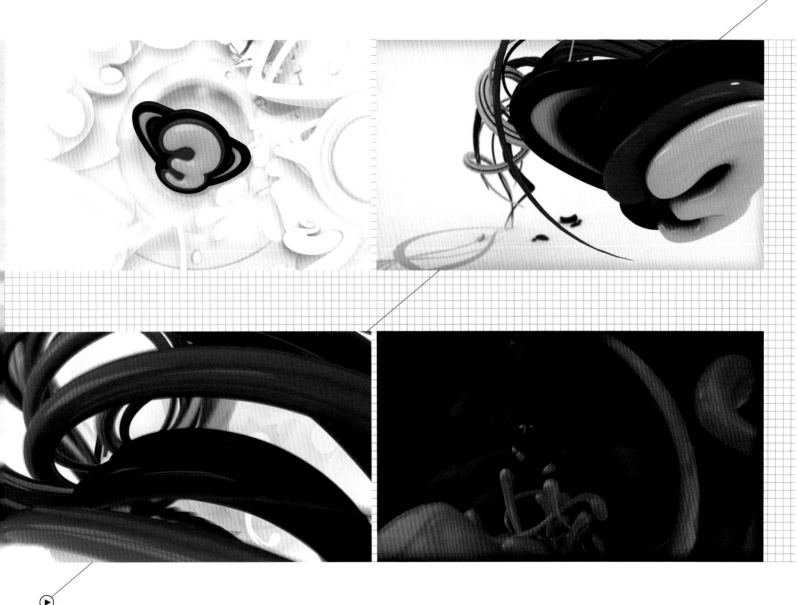

**Project:** Canal Super3 Channel ID

**Art Direction:** Inocuo the Sign;
**3D / Animation:** Physalia;
**Compositing:** Hugo Basism;
**Client:** Canal Super3;
**Software:** 3ds Max & After Effects.

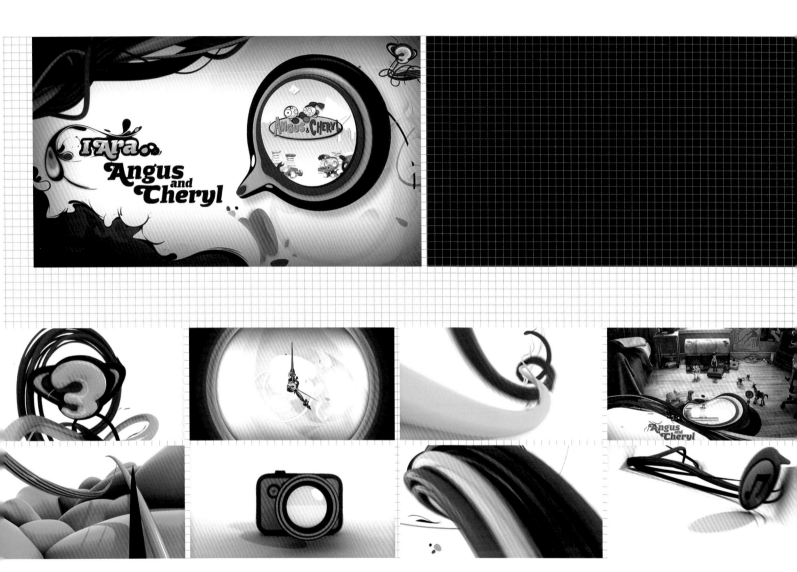

These series of bugs and idents are created to engage young audiences for a long period of time, so special effort is put into creating something fun and vibrant in order to catch kids' eyes. The aim of this design is to make every frame funny and interesting.

**Project:** Adobe Photoshop Cook

**Design Firm:** Minimalbaroque;
**Designer:** Maya Rota Klein;
**Client:** Adobe Young GC Contest;
**Software:** Photoshop & Premiere.

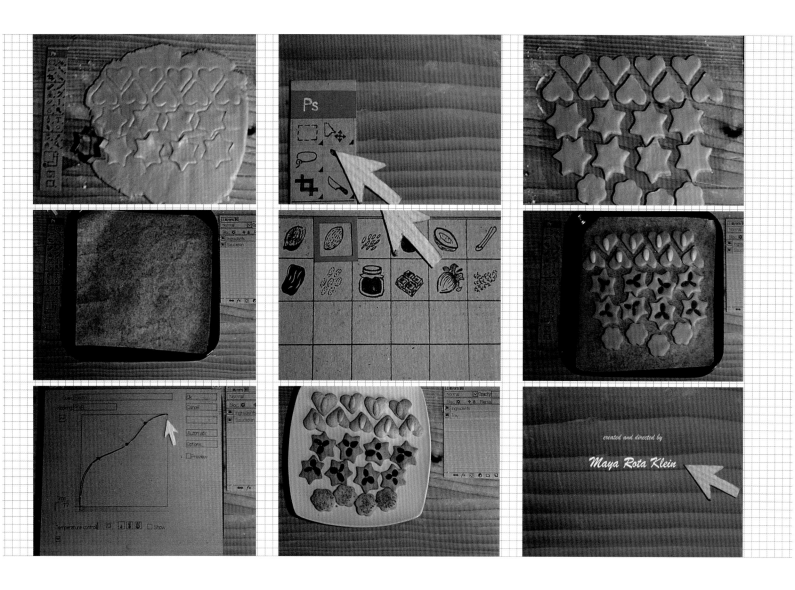

The video made in stop-motion for competition AdobeYouGC shows how to make the lovely butter cookies with the new Adobe Photoshop Cook. The whole set is made with cardboard and kitchen utensils. The work is designed to continue the research concerning virtual and material, cold and hot. The "coldness" of digital work is softened by the "warmth" of craftsman. The kitchen takes us more than three dimensions in the two-dimensional monitor that offers other dimensions – the dimension of time (or time of the memories) that is a daily activity like cooking and the fragmentation of time that is an essential characteristic of stop-motion and the emotional dimension that refers to the usage of materials, sounds and colors as well as the movements of the subjects.

**Project:** On Screen

**Design Firm:** Drool Studio;
**Designers:** Jorge Artola, Fernando Navarro, Edu Martinéz;
**Client:** Zoopy TV;
**Software:** Illustrator, Photoshop, After Effects, Premiere, Cinema 4D.

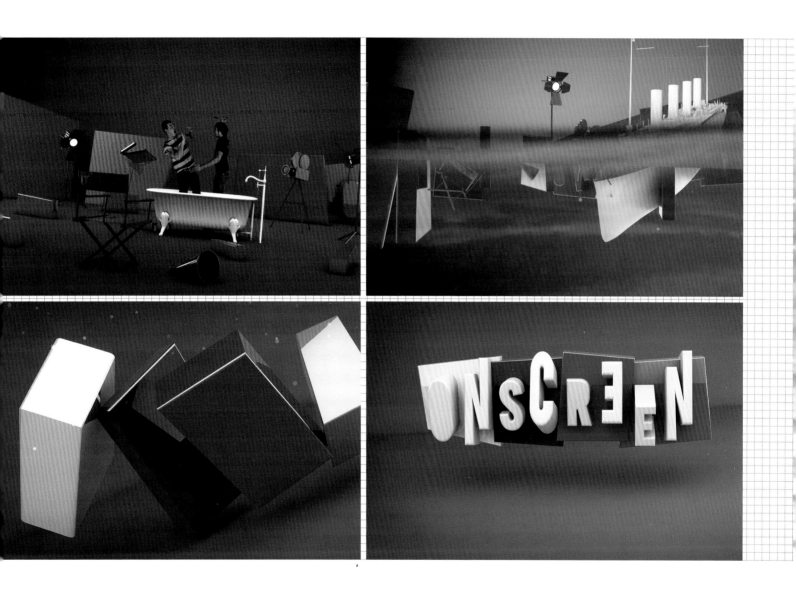

This unique motion design is designed by the cooperation of Drool Studio and Zoopy TV on the Re-brand & Idents Package for their movie review TV Show: "On Screen", which is hosted by Jay & Dave. The whole design mixes real people and cartoon settings together to construct sequent interesting frames.

**Project:** DPMX (Diseño Punto MX)

**Design Firm:** Tridente Brand Firm;
**Designer:** Alejandro Uzeta;
**Client:** ITESM (Instituto Tecnológico y de Estudios Superiores de Monterrey);
**Software:** Boujou, Cinema 4D, After Effects, Illustrator, Photoshop, Soundtrack Pro, Pro Tools.

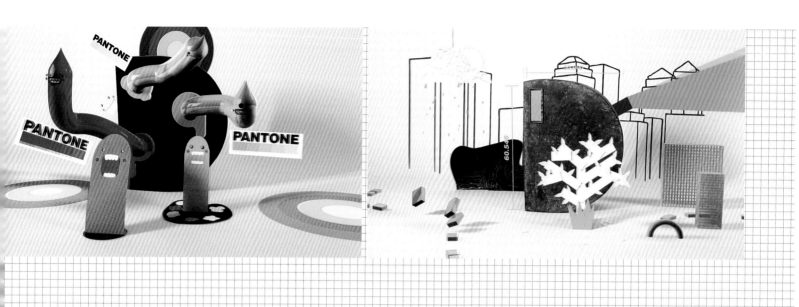

ALBERTOVILLARREAL·ARIELR
OJO·BEGUIRISTÁIN·BERGERA·
CARMÉPINÓS·DANNYVENLET·
ÉXODO·JEREMYVICKERY·JOS
EPHGILLAND·NATHANSHEDR
OFF·PASCALARQUITECTOS·P
HILFRANK·ROBERTGREENWO
OD·RODORAMIREZ

The concept of DPMX is developed in Tridente. It is related on 3 Ds (Development, Design, Digital), so the design team made 3 real Ds and shot the videos with curve rails for a 3D anaglyph effect that can be seen with a red-cyan lens. There is no 3D plug-in used in this production. The music is composed in Tridente too, and the recording and mixing is made by Claudio Ramírez.

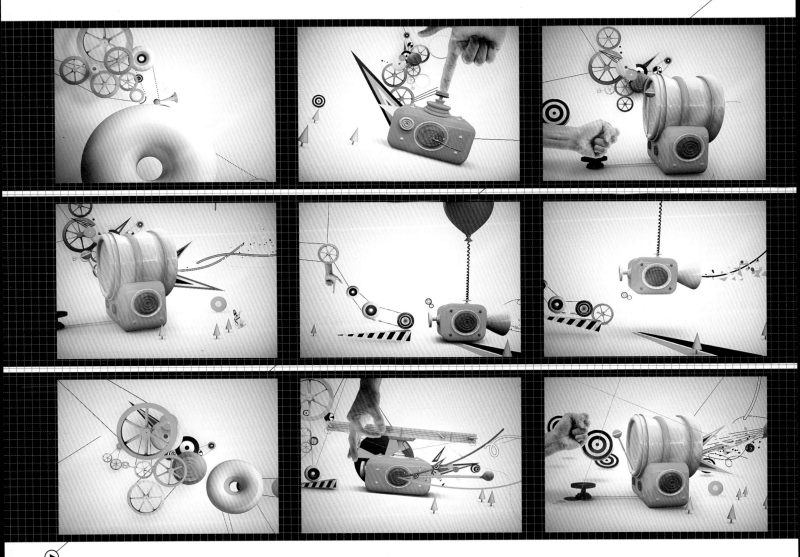

**Project:** Estudio VH1

**Design Firm:** MTV Design Services Latam + Hola Mambo;
**Creative Director:** Camilo Barría;
**Directors:** Camilo Barría & Luis Suarez;
**Designers:** Camilo Barría, Luis Suarez, Martín Muerza, Adriana Campos;
**Client:** MTV Networks Latinamerica;
**Audio:** Facilmusic;
**Software:** After Effects, Cinema 4D, Photoshop.

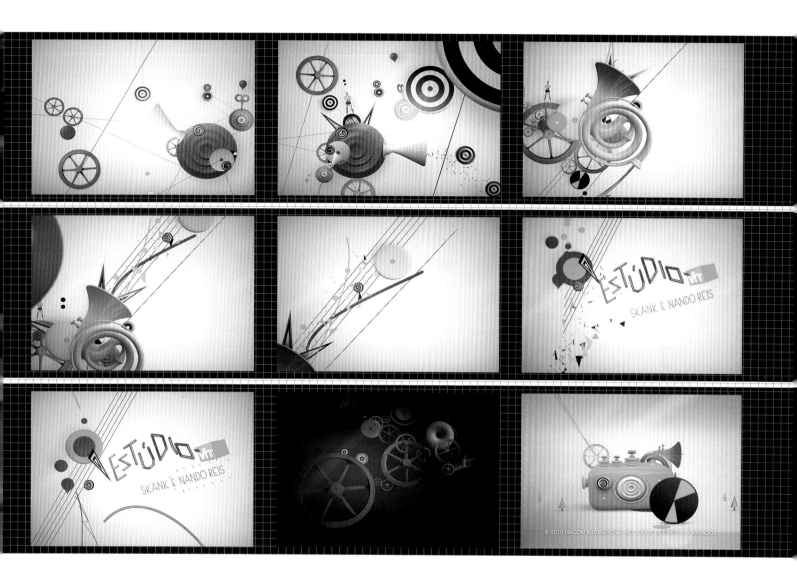

The collage of machines and humans in this short film is to represent a perfect mix of musicians from different backgrounds that come together each week in this new TV show on VH1. Just to make some machines, make noise, and make friends.

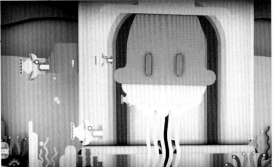

**Project:** Stories from the Neighbourhood

**Design Firm:** The Neighbourhood;
**Designer / Director:** Jon Humphreys;
**Animation:** Tim Woods, Stuart Dearaley;
**Software:** 3ds Max, Illustrator, Photoshop, After Effects, Premiere.

This is a self-promotion film of the motion design firm The Neighbourhood. It is created to celebrate some of the things that influence pop-up story books, retro robots and tiki culture. It is designed in Illustrator first, then transferred into 3D and textured and lit to give an analogue handmade feel at last.

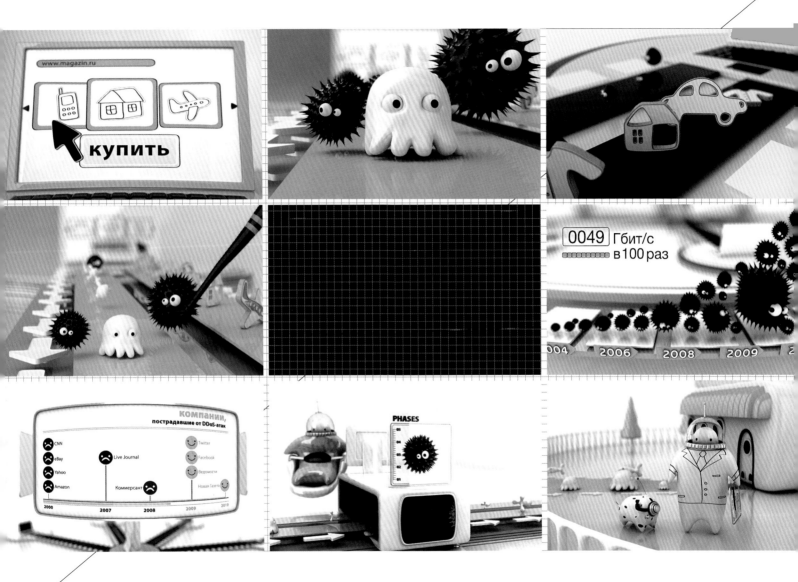

**Project**: Orange Cartoon

**Design Firm:** Mercator Group;
**Executive Producer:** Andrey Skvortsov;
**Art-Director:** Nonna Khismatullina;
**Client:** Orange Business Services;
**Software:** After Effects, Premiere, 3ds Max, Photoshop, Illustrator.

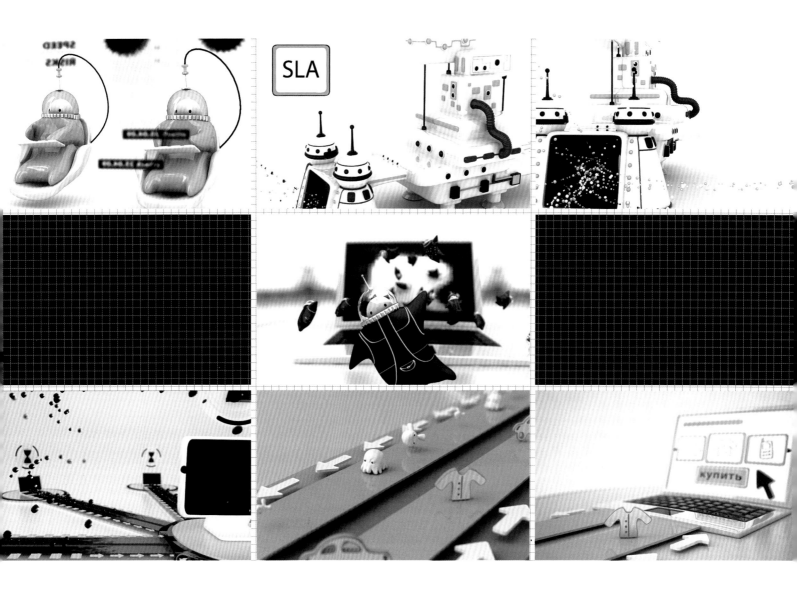

This project presents the new service from Orange Company. The characters, like the orange rescuers, ordinary users, useful signals, cruel monsters and other heroes of the virtual space, explain what DDoS-attacks are and how to deal with them easily and vividly.

▶**Project:** TRTÉ Channel Brand

**Design Firm:** RTÉ Graphic Design Department;
**Designers:** Alan Dunne & Stephen McNally;
**Client:** RTÉ Television, Ireland;
**Software:** After Effects, SoftImage, Flame.

FINE TUNING

The aim of the work is to develop a channel brand for the often elusive adolescent or "tween" audience. The branding's visual style is informed by the way Irish teenagers like to customize their schoolbags and pencil cases with intensely detailed pen doodles. The chosen style is madcap, fun and irreverent pen illustrations with a minimal color palette. Particularly detailed animations allow for new surprises each time. The hand-drawn approach and idiosyncratic approach stand out as a brash contrast to competitors' ident designs that have huge budgets. There are over 1,500 hand-rendered illustrations during the animation process.

**Project**: Dérapage

**Design Firm:** Benoit Massé;
**Designers:** Benoit Massé & Rosalie Pepin;
**Software:** After Effects, Photoshop.

This is a short stop-motion for the 10th anniversary of Dérapage, a non-narrative film festival. The idea behind the ten hand-made cupcakes is to revisit the countdown and celebrate the festival at the same time.

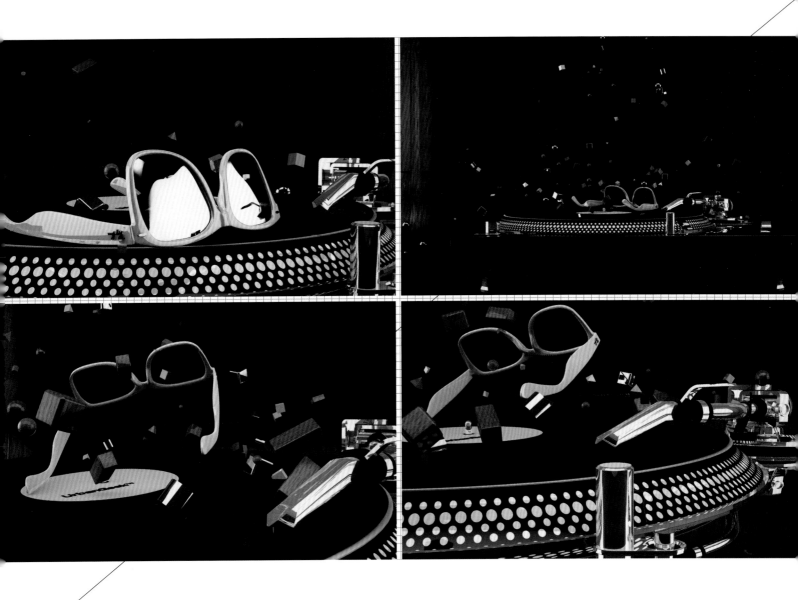

## Project: UrbanGeek

**Design Firm:** UrbanGeek;
**Designer:** Michael Fawke;
**Software:** After Effects & Cinema 4D.

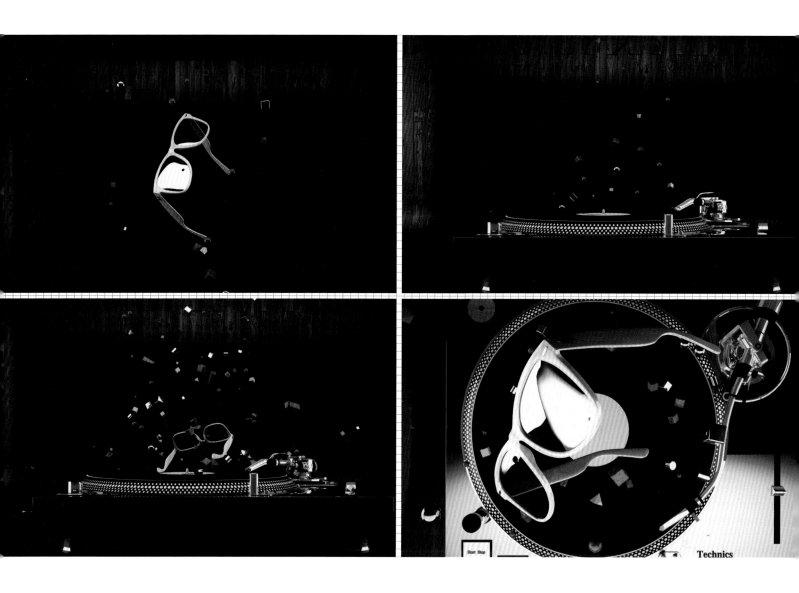

This is a self-directed university project by Michael Fawke of BA (Hons) Graphic Design.
It is also a self-promotional visual – the objects and materials represent the design, the
wayfarers and the turntable reflect the influences of the designer.

## Actop

Location: Barcelona, Spain
Email: actop@actop.net
Web: www.actop.net

Actop is a creative cell based in Barcelona and formed by Alvaro P. Posadas & César Pesquera. They operate as an open structure experimenting and collaborating with different agencies, collectives and artists and working on a wide range of media: print, animation, motion graphics, live visuals and new approaches to the moving image.

## Alan Dunne

Location: Dublin, Ireland
Tel: +353 85 7198589
Email: alandunnedesign@gmail.com
Web: www.be.net/AlanDunne; www.vimeo.com/AlanDunne

Alan Dunne is a motion designer, illustrator and art director living in Dublin, Ireland. He graduated from NCAD in 2005 with a BDes in Visual Communications. He has received various awards for his motion design work from the Irish Design Institute (IDI) and has also taken part in the ICAD Upstarts programme in advertising. He has designed and art directed many motion design and live action sequences for RTÉ Television, Ireland's national broadcaster. They range from title designs, station idents, documentary content graphics and promotional designs.

## Alfredo Villa

Location: Distrito Federal, Mexico
Email: botecual@hotmail.com
Web: www.be.net/alfredin

Mexican Graphic Designer, 25 years old, Alfredo Villa studied in UNAM FES Acatlan. After 4 years of studies, he collaborated in freelance work with Film Mates Graph, a TV company producer dedicated to making a lot of graphics for Mexican TV shows. After 3 freelance projects, Alfredo Villa worked full time for 6 months. In this company, Alfredo Villa won a Promax BDA Silver Drama Promotion.

## Amine Alameddine

Address: Achrafieh Street, Beirut / Lebanon
Tel: +961 1 217 147
Web: www.caustik.tv

Amine is a motion graphic and broadcast designer who specializes in branding and 3D animation for TV commercials and TV channels. He gathered skills in both architecture and graphic design, trained and worked in Lebanon and the U.K until he recently founded "Caustik", which caters to an array of clients from around the globe. He lectures at the ALBA / Balamand campus in computer graphics and animation.

## Andrey Muratov

Location: Moscow, Russia
Tel: +7 915 081 87 66
Email: proxell.tv@gmail.com
Web: www.proxell.tv

Andrey Muratov is a director of a post production studio based in Moscow, Russia. He graduated from the Humanitarian Institute of Television and Broadcasting, and has 7 years experience in direction, motion & TV design, interactive (web, flash) design, film production & postproduction, game industry and photography. He has worked with many brands, such as: Nike, Lancôme, L'Oréal, Microsoft (Russia), MasterCard (Russia), RZD (Russia), Mercedes-Benz, FerreroRocher and Marussia | Auto (Frankfurt IAA 2009 Germany).

## ANTI

Address: Kristian Augusts gate 13, 0164 Oslo, Norway; Sandviksveien 62b, 5035 Bergen, Norway
Tel: +47 934 45 238; +47 916 27 586
Email: post@anti.as
Web: www.anti-ink.com

Anti is a multi-disciplinary design agency that works with brand identity, art direction, packaging, print, illustration and interactive design. Anti believes in the power of developing visual languages. They provide clients not only with aesthetic graphic solutions, but with a visual voice that provides relevant and successful solutions to who they are and what they want to achieve. Anti has a broad diversity in client experience from dairy / soft drinks, lifestyle, culture, telecom to art and advertising agencies. In addition to their clients Anti provides advertising agencies with the best possible solutions in visual application and in particular online digital solutions.

## Ari Kruger

Address: 4 Loop Str, Studio 1002, Cape Town, South Africa
Tel: +27 82 376 7648
Web: www.sktchbk.com

Ari Kruger, the founder of Sketchbook Studios, has been working in animation and visual effects for eight years, freelancing for post production houses both in Cape Town and Sydney. Ari is also a filmmaker who writes and directs short films which usually feature both live action and visual effects, which he does all himself. His short film FOCUS was selected as a finalist for Tropfest, the world's largest short film festival, which takes place every year in Australia.

## Artur Jurzyk

Location: Warsaw, Poland
Tel: +48 790 024 990
Web: www.ar2.com.pl

Artur "ar2" Jurzyk is a creative motion designer, director and producer born in Warsaw in 1983. He is an innovator in the field of visual techniques. Back when nobody knew that Facebook existed, Artur had already realized his first steps in "mapping 3D technology". Since 2004 he has constantly worked with passion as a VJ ar2 in Warsaw's underground clubs, galleries and festivals. He gained priceless experience whilst working for the biggest international TV stations like MTV Networks and Fashion TV. Artur was also featured in Polish National Television (TVP), Polsat channel and for plenty marketing agencies. Nowadays, with his fellow media makers, Artur is developing a new studio Gagarin.pl.

## Benoit Massé

Location: Montreal, Québec, Canada
Tel: + 1 514 582 1257
Email: bmasse@utopiko.com
Web: www.utopiko.com

Benoit Massé is a multi-disciplinary designer. He completed a bachelor's degree in Graphic Design in 2006 and has been a professional freelancer ever since, working in the field of motion and web design, illustrations and art direction. His love for movement and interactivity is leading him to a Graduate Certificate in Computation Arts.

## Binalogue

Location: Madrid, Spain
Tel: +34 912 509 849
Email: kontakto@binalogue.com
Web: www.binalogue.com

Binalogue is a cross-disciplinary design studio founded in Australia with established branches in America, Europe and Australia. Their steadily growing team is comprised of talented and passionate members from all corners of the world, constantly pushing their boundaries and looking at each project as uniquely challenging and fun. With design as their starting point, they direct and develop creative content and communication solutions for a wide range of media, focusing on broadcast (network branding, motion graphics, VFX) and online (interactive design & development) platforms. Their participation in the various projects they undertake depends on their clients' needs. Whether it is at the concept development stage or at any special phase, they work closely with them to produce quality end results that meet their high standards while having a great experience in the process.

## Birg

Location: Oost-Vlaanderen, Belgium
Email: birg@birg.be
Web: www.birg.bo

Birg is a motion graphics designer and Art director. He studied art from 1992-1996 and cinematography from 1996-2000. He was in Colorist at Color by Dejonghe from 2000-2003, and worked as a freelance editor and animator from 2003-2007, then as an art director and animator at thefridge.tv. Currently he works as a freelance art director and animator.

## Cafundó Estúdio

Location: Florianópolis, SC, Brazil
Tel: +55 48 3235 1030
Email: contato@cafundó.tv
Web: www.cafundó.tv

Since 2008, located in Florianópolis, SC, Brazil, Cafundó has been a creative studio and a vibrant space, where the colors of creativity shine in the swirl of awesome ideas. Talent, technology and professionalism are the house's best in an environment that resonates innovation. Their atmosphere filled with design, motion graphics, digital brand activation and offline interactions will transform your gaze on the universe of communication.

## Cai Griffith

Location: Epsom, UK
Tel: +44 791 781 0434
Web: www.caigriffith.com

Cai Griffith is a Graphic and New Media designer & recent graduate of the University for the Creative Arts, Epsom. He is interested in unusual forms of image making and how these analog processes can be digitized to create unique pieces of work. Alongside motion graphics he also has a great love for traditional print media; Cai Griffith thinks there is a lot to learn from traditional Graphic Design, aspects which are relevant across all modern mediums.

## Camilo Barría Royer

Location: Buenos Aires, Argentina.
Tel: +54 11 48027840
Web: www.thegogogo.tv

Camilo Barria Royer is a self-taught Director and Art Director. Born in Chile, raised in Venezuela and now living in Buenos Aires is the perfect example of Latin America mixture and chaos. Now he leads the Mtv Design Services Latam Team as its Creative Director and Director for all the region but also developing projects for Mtv world feeds like Asia and Europe. Graduated in Sociology from Universidad Central de Venezuela and with an MA in Type and Design from Universidad Católica de Chile now spends his time between images and sounds. With 13 years of experience he worked in broadcast design at places such as HBO Latin American Group, Chilevision and animation studio Punga Visual Consorcio. During his career Camilo Barria has won silver and gold awards at the Promax/BDA Conference in the fields of Best On Screen Type, Best Show Open, Best On Air Identity Campaign and Best On Air Program Packaging, and has been published several times in the worldwide-recognized motion magazine *Stash*.

## Candaş Şişman

Location: Istanbul, Turkey
Tel: +905 057610475
Web: www.csismn.com

Candaş Şişman (born in zmir, 1985) graduated from Eskisehir Anatolian University Animation Department after finishing izmir Anatolian Fine Arts High School, During his undergraduate studies he took multimedia design education for one year in Netherlands. In 2009 he founded Silo 1 with his friends. Since 2006 he has received many awards such as Rome Viedram Festival Video and Sound Design best prize, Apple I-can competition best animation prize and he has participated in many important festivals like Olympia Experimental Music Festival and Nemo Digital Arts and Film Festival. Candaş Şişman recently realized Yekpare projection mapping with Deniz Kader and NERDWORKING within Istanbul 2010 European Capital of Culture activities and performed Stereoscopic Audiovisual among Babylon Audiovisual Monday activities.

## Carlo Vega

Location: New York, USA
Email: cv@carlovega.com
Web: www.carlovega.com

Carlo Vega is a creative director, animator, artist and photographer born in Lima, Peru, and now based in New York City. He began his professional work experience as a graphic designer while obtaining his college degree. He has since collaborated with world-renowned advertising agencies, brands and design studios. Vega works with clients such as AOL, BCBG, Best Buy, CMT, Victoria's Secret, Nike and NBC, among others. His commercial projects have been shown in animation festivals in addition to earning industry awards and recognition. His personal artwork, animation style and distinctive imagery are highly regarded and have been featured in group exhibitions around the globe.

## Cento Lodigiani

Location: Via Pistrucci 6, Milano, Italy
Tel: +0039 3479220330
Web: www.centolodigiani.com

Cento Lodigiani is an eclectic Italian motion designer based in Milan. Even before obtaining a degree in communication deign at Politecnico di Milano he started to work in the fields of illustration, videos, motion graphics, logo treatments, digital arts, design for music industry.

## CENTOUNOPERCENTO

Address: via Luigi Biolchini 21a 00146 Rome, Italy
Email: ciao@centounopercento.com
Web: www.centounopercento.com

Centounopercento is a collective of visual artist, bringing together skills from different backgrounds. They act as a creative consultancy, providing intelligent solutions to match the unique demands of every project. They work collaboratively and individually and assemble specific top talent teams according to produtions. Centounopercento is mainly focused in the area of motion, across tv, cinema, promos, commercials, web, live events and new technologies. From graphics to visual FX, from animation to sound design they are constantly developing new projects, pushing the boundaries of design to ensure high quality work, which sets their clients apart from the market.

## Chaidalis Constantinos

Location: Athens, Greece
Email: brittlemail@gmail.com
Web: www.brittle.gr

Chaidalis Constantinos (aka Brittle) is a Greek self-taught graphic & motion broadcast designer with a background in industrial design and arts. Chaidalis had owned Onedotzero 2006 Athens (First Prize Winner) Ebge award (best intro video) Ebge Merit (editorial illustration) Independent film festival selection EXHIBITIONS FESTIVALS Cheap Art, Onedotzero, MTV Playground, Moscow graphic design biennale, SFFF, Athens Video Art Festival, Reworks 2009, Digital Poetry HAFF,REWORKS and many more.

## Diego Soto Aguirre

Location: Madrid, Spain
Email: Diego.szcrew@gmail.com
Web: www.behance.net/kinseartworks

Diego Soto Aguirre is a member of Kinseartworks, a Spanish art director born in Madrid in 1987. He graduated from the Escuela Superior de Publicidad in 2009. He is the winner of the contest for the logo for the 150th anniversary of Santa Teresa, with publications in books like *Select H* from Index Book and *Generation X* of Alvaro Perez.

## DI-T

Location: London, England
Email: i@di-t.com
Web: www.di-t.com

Dimo Trifonov is a 21-year-old Bulgarian artist currently based in London. He has almost 6 years in the design trip. Started with Illustration & Graphic Design, now he is doing motion graphics,

video and photography too. Proud member of Keystone Design Union and Society27. He also has a few years of experience in advertising.

## DEUBAL-Olivier Marquézy

Location: Paris, French
Tel: +01 42 52 21 27
Web: www.deubal.com

Olivier Marquezy is part of Deubal, a Paris-based studio founded with Stéphanie Lelong, specializing in illustration-based motion design, print and animation. Their work is often character-based and also highly focused on typography, which he designs sometimes for the specific needs of a project. He studied graphic design for print in school and then learned video and animation while working for a few years with animation duo Kuntzel+Deygas, with whom he created the titles for Spielberg's "Catch me if you can". Deubal created a few TV brand identities and TV titles for the German-French network Arte, Canal+, France Télévision, as well as film title sequences, short films, ads, music videos, children's books, poster designs, T-shirts and set design.

## Deniz Kader

Location: Istanbul, Turkey
Email: deniskader@gmail.com
Web: www.csismn.com

Deniz Kader (born in Bulgaria, 1983), after finishing zmir Anatolian Fine Arts High School, graduated from Eski ehir Anatolian University Animation Department. During his undergraduate studies he took multimedia design education for one year in Netherlands. In 2009 he founded Silo 1 with his friends. Since 2006 he has participated in many important festivals. Deniz Kader recently realized Yekpare projection mapping with Candaş Şişman and Nerdworking within stanbul 2010 European Capital of Culture activities and performed Stereoscopic Audiovisual among Babylon Audiovisual Monday activities.

## Drool Studio

Location: Madrid, Spain
Email: hello@droolstudio.com
Web: www.droolstudio.com

Drool Studio stems from its founder's needs of making really creative projects that merge an attractive / functional communication with a visual impact. The studio is based in the heart of Madrid, Spain. They create their works with passion and impulse their professional and personal goals. When a client presents them a project in Drool, they always try to get involved in their ambient and corporative culture. At the same time they like the client to be part of the process, in that way the final product will be really impressive.

## Dvein

Location: Barcelona, Spain
Tel: +34931822844
Web: www.dvein.com

Dvein is a motion and interactive studio based in Barcelona. They provide art direction, design and animation for cinema, broadcast, music videos, etc. They get involved in any given step in the creative process from the concept art and story boarding to the final piece in projects involving video or interactive.

## Eat My Dear

Location: Vienna, Austria
Tel: +43 (0) 1 966 07 10; Fax: +43 (0) 1 403 45 57
Email: info@eatmydear.com
Web: www.eatmydear.com

Eat My Dear is a motion design studio founded by the two designers/directors Markus Hornof and Patrick Sturm in 2005. The studio, located in Vienna, Austria, focuses on motion design for advertising, broadcast as well as in-store animations.
Their responsibilities include concept development and production of both live action and animated commercials/short films, as well as multimedia events, while managing the workflow in all stages of production to ensure flawless communication between directors, writers, concept artists and clients.

## Emedialab

Location: Malaga, Spain
Tel: +34 952210307; Fax: +34 952225787
Web: www.emedialab.es

EMedialab is an independent company founded in 2006 aiming to create and develop audiovisual projects. During these years EMedialab has worked with companies such as JWT Delvico Spain, Price Waterhouse Coopers, Universal Music Spain, Málaga Spanish Film Festival and Andalusian Tourism Office, amongst others.

## Eugene and Louise

Location: Oost-Vlaanderen, Belgium
Email: info@eugene-and-louise.com
Web: www.eugene-and-louise.com

Eugene and Louise is a Belgium-based creative studio founded by Glenn D'Hondt and Sylvia Meert. E&L focuses on character design, illustration and original content. A contemporary & appealing look with lots of heart-conquering characters, catchy story lines and some belly-shaking humor, all wrapped up in an innovative graphic style are what makes Eugene and Louise stand out.

## Frank Sauer

Location: Darmstadt, Germany
Tel: +0049 163 770 65 35
Email: contact@frank-sauer.com
Web: www.frank-sauer.com

Frank Sauer is a director, designer and animator located in Darmstadt, Germany, near Frankfurt. With 4 years commercial experience his clients include SAT1, BBC, Discovery Channel and a lot more. Frank Sauer graduated as a Master of Media Direction from the University of Applied Sciences Darmstadt in 2009.

## Jalea.tv

Location: Buenos Aires, Argentina
Tel: +54 11 4778 1166
Web: www.jalea.tv

Jalea.tv is a boutique art-motion studio from Buenos Aires, Argentina. Founded in 2008 by Luis Goldberg and Valeria Laura Rapoport, two audiovisual designers who after working for a variety of Argentinian studios for several years, decided to follow their hunger for exploration and growths and create a place where they could continue their never-ending search with freedom.

Having worked for clients such as MTV, Sony, Fox, Lifestyle, Movistar, Axe, Nike, Pringles and Ford, been part of shows and projection mappings. Their works were also featured in many art shows.

## Joao Lucas

Location: Lisbon, Portugal
Email: joao.goncalo.lucas@gmail.com
Web: www.behance.net/jlucas

Joao Lucas is a 21-year-old motion designer and recently graduated in Multimedia Art from the Faculty of Fine Arts of Lisbon. Currently he is studying at Arqui300 Academy in 3D and Film Production. He is passionate about design, photography, video, and 3D and he tries to integrate a little bit of everything in his work.

## Jonas Strandberg Ringh

Add: Samaritgand 4, 118 53 Stockholm, Sweden
Tel: +46 739 22 29 80
Web: www.cubadust.com

Jonas Strandberg-Ringh is a Swedish graphic designer with a background in fine arts. Studying at two of Stockholm most recognized art schools gave him a great eye for color and composition, something that has been of great use while working in the digital field as a graphic designer. Cubadust.com is a well respected name in the online design scene partly due to Jonas's success in both non-commercial and professional work. This has given him the opportunity to appear in both online and live events such as the International Word and Image Conference, Corels Digital Art Exhibition Tour, The Third Place – Playstation – Digital Expressions and also be featured in numerous books and magazine publications.

## Jonathan Gurvit

Location: Buenos Aires, Argentina
Email: jonathan.gurvit@gmail.com
Web: www.be.net/JonathanGurvit

Jonathan Gurvit started his career in February 2000. He joined DDB Argentina as a Junior Art Director and worked for clients such as Telefónica, Volkswagen, Exxon, Clorox, ING, Bank Boston, Energizer & Danone. In 2004 Jonathan became Creative Director at Del Campo Nazca Saatchi & Saatchi and developed the "Pampers.com" campaign, which won, among other awards, Pampers first Cannes Lion. After more than 10 years working at creative agencies, in 2011, he decided to start a new career, this time as a film director. During his career Jonathan Gurvit has won 10 Cannes Lions, 15 Clios, and more than 200 awards in One Show, D&AD, New York Festivals (Grand Prix), Ojo de Iberoamerica, FIAP & CCCA.

## Jorge Artola

Location: Madrid, Spain
Email: yo@jorgeartola.com
Web: www.jorgeartola.com

Based in the heart of Madrid, Spain, Jorge Artola is a Panamanian graphic / motion designer, art director & occasional illustrator working on advertising, broadcast and digital media. Since high school, Jorge has been exploring different elements in the world of art, even if it moves or not. From directing a music video to creating a new typography, he's always trying to find the right balance between aesthetics and practicality.

## Julie Ruiz

Location: New York, USA
Email: juliebluelovesyou@gmail.com
Web: www.julieruiz.com

Julie Ruiz is the director of the off-air Design team at VH1 in New York City. She also works as a freelance designer and a photographer specializing in musicians and live shows. Her work has been featured in and recognized by *AIGA, PRINT, Communication Arts, PDN, LE BOOK, BDA*, notcot.org, *the One Show, HOW, CTAM* and *Creativity*.
Julie Ruiz grew up in the small town of Eureka Springs, Arkansas. She was inspired by teenage boredom and rebellion, whether she was carving on park benches or spray painting her VW bus, art was always a natural part of her life.
She eventually escaped to the Art Institute of Ft. Lauderdale, where after many packs of ramen noodles and countless hours at Kinkos she received her design degree in 2000. She landed her first job at MTV Latin America and then in 2002 found her sweet home in New York City and at VH1, where she is currently Design Director.

## Junaid-Ur-Rehman

Location: Lahore, Pakistan
Email: junaid_tm@hotmail.com
Web: www.vimeo.com/junaid; www.behance.net/junaidcreative

Junaid Jamil a motion graphics artist in Pakistan. He worked in various renowned TV channels of Pakistan, such as CNBC Pakistan, AAJ NEWS and Rung Television. Now he is working for DUNYA News. He has five years of work experience in 2D and 3D animation using the current industry standard tools.

## Hola Mambo

Location: Buenos Aires, Argentina.
Tel: +54 11 48027840
Web: www.holamambo.com

Hola Mambo is a tiny cute motion design boutique formed in Buenos Aires by Luis Suarez and Cony Aravena. Creatively directed by Luis Suarez, Hola Mambo focuses on searching for new ways to understand broadcast design and animation, always prioritizing a good sense of humor, rhythm, good looks and rebellion with a classic design approach.
Luis Suarez has been working in Santiago de Chile and Buenos Aires in motion design and animation since 2000 with clients like MTV, VH1, TBS, NatGeo, Voyage, HBO and the animation studio SMOG, and so on.

## Ilias Sounas

Location: Athens, Greece
Email: ilias@sounasdesign.com
Web: www.sounasdesign.com

Ilias Sounas is a self-taught Greek illustrator / 2D animator working under the name of Sounas Design. He has provided illustrations, character animations and fresh motion graphics for various projects since 2007.
His personal animated stories which feature fresh character design and flash-based animation have been awarded and nominated in various festivals worldwide. Ilias Sounas currently provides graphics and animations for games in various mobile platforms.

## Kike del Mar

Location: México City, Mexico
Email: ans_fa@hotmail.com
Web: www.behance.net/kikedelmar

Born in México City and 28 years old, Kike del Mar studied in UAM Azc. Between 2003 & 2007, he started working in "Once TV México", working as a Junior Motion Designer for Once Niños, the kids space of the channel. From late 2008 until today, he has worked in "Mvs Televisión" as a Senior Motion Designer. In 2009, Kike del Mar won Promax BDA, World Gold Rocket Award.

## King and Country

Address: 1808 Stanford st. Santa Monica, CA 90404
Tel: 310-586-0100; Fax: 310-586-0101
Web: www.kingandcountry.tv

King AND Country is a commercial production and design company specializing in Motion Graphics, 3D Animation and Live Action. They communicate and collaborate through the union of graphic design, live action filmmaking, animation, visual effects and other creative content. Sometimes they are brought on to help brand an empire, other times they're asked to tell a great story. The studio approaches each job with the clients' needs in mind and strives to keep the creation unfiltered and pure.

## KORB

Location: Vilnius, Lithuania
Tel: +37069876775
Web: www.korb.lt

KORB is a freelance-based VFX and design company founded by CGI director Rimantas Lukavicius. Working along with other freelancers and companies KORB specifies in visual effects, motion graphics and mixed media projects. KORB has been bringing ideas to motion since 2005.

## Lichtfaktor

Address: Zuelpicher Strasse 28, 50674 Cologne, Germany
Tel: +49 221 80158085
Web: www.lichtfaktor.eu

The members of Lichtfaktor use light to give expression to their creativity. They take advantage of a variety of light sources to produce photos and videos in cities by night. The Cologne artists' collective, consisting of VJ $ehvermögen (photographer and VJ), Visionlabz (Programmer and VJ), JIAR (communications designer and graffiti artist) and Daniel Lisson (communications designer and graphic designer), experiments with the possibilities yielded by bulb (long-term) exposure and painting. The team's aim is to explore many aspects of "lightwriting" and to develop it further.

## ManvsMachine

Location: London, UK
Tel: +44 (0)20 7613 2040
Web: http://manvsmachine.co.uk

ManvsMachine is a design & motion studio based in London, England. Since opening its doors in early 2007, ManvsMachine has grown into a multi-award winning, multinational team of creative specialists directing & producing globally acclaimed branding, commercials, animation, film & print.

## Marblart

Location: Utrecht, the Netherlands
Tel: +0031 64 575 2332
Web: www.marblart.com

Marblart is a cross media creative production studio based in Utrecht, the Netherlands. The team creates and produces still and moving images. Marblart is specialized in traditional and digital 2D animation, graphics for all media, compositing and video productions, and creates content from start to complete production, all in one house.

## MateriaBlanca – Estudio Visual

Location: Medellin, Colombia
Email: materialanca@gmail.com
Web: www.vimeo.com/materiablanca

Materiablanca – Visual Studio is a selection of creators and generators' creative ideas represented through animation, multimedia and photography. It started when two great friends and fellow academics in the city of Medellin and Colombia decided to form a work group where their most outrageous and outlandish ideas could be found with the concepts from clients, and it is possible to bring different and innovative proposals together. They have designed many clean yet powerful and psychedelic productions which take the audience to a high-end visual impact.

## Maya Rota Klein

Location: Turin, Italy
Email: myminimalbaroque@gmail.com
Web: www.minimalbaroque.com

Born in Udine in 1984, Stefania Rota alias Maya Rota Klein graduated from the IED (Europe Institute of Design) in Turin in digital and virtual design. She is a video artist and director specializing in stop motion, animation, experimental and research of new languages. Currently she is working as a director and artist at minimalbaroque.com. She worked as creative journalist at kinematrix for the 68th Venice Film Festival and photographer at Rototom Sunsplash European Reggae Festival before. She won the critic's prize from Adobe and the critics' prize Grinzane Cavour on new technologies. She is recognized as one of "the new talents of video art" by Flash Art International.

## MEMOMA

Location: Ciudad de Mexico, Mexico
Tel: +52 (555) 5338181
Web: www.memoma.tv

MEMOMA STUDIO explores visual culture from different disciplines to create breathtaking imagery for TV, entertainment, brands, advertising and music industry through motion graphics, design, art and live direction.

## Mercator Group

Location: Moscow, Russia
Tel: +7 (495) 788-8906
Web: www.mercator.ru

Mercator Group specializes in the presentation of ideas, products, businesses, and information. Mercator Group is a leading team in production of information graphics, presentations, and videos, the operative word being "information". They never produce works void of content on principle. On the other hand, they can present information in a simple and understandable manner, convincingly and vividly, dryly or emotionally, humorously or without humor, elegantly, using rigorous or careless style, inconspicuously – in a word, the way the client need it.

## Mirari&Co (mirari.tv)

Location: Sydney, Australia
Email: info@mirari.tv
Web: www.mirari.tv

Mirari&Co. is a new multi-disciplinary design studio which specializes in high-end design and production in all media including motion (film, TV), print and interactive design. Founded in 2010, Mirari&Co. has been refreshing the industry through innovative concepts and dynamic animation. Their mission is to discover unique design solutions through multiple, creative approaches. By integrating elements inspired by the world around them, Mirari&Co. is able to generate new ideas and bring a fresh distinctive personality to a brand. They are a strong, cohesive unit of directors, designers and animators can transform a concept into a beautiful imagery. They always bring honesty, structural integrity and a fire for new ideas.

## Murat Pak

Location: Turkey
Email: undream@undream.net
Web: www.undream.net

As the founder of UNDREAM, Murat Pak is a passionate dreamer of the postmodern era. UNDREAM is an international multi-award-winning studio crafting inspiration for all media experiences. UNDREAM has been featured in various societies like *Shots*, *Stash*, *Motionographer*, *Graphic Design*, *Computer Arts*, *CGSocieties*, *Vimeo* besides numerous other magazines, festivals, publications and installations.

## Nate Londa

Location: Savannah, USA
Email: natelonda@gmail.com
Web: www.natelonda.com

Nate Londa is a recent graduate of Savannah College of Art & Design with a BFA in Motion Media Design and a minor in Graphic Design. He enjoys exploring and experimenting to creatively solve problems and generate innovative ideas. He is looking forward to getting into the industry and continuing to push the boundaries on design, aesthetics, and motion media.

## NERDWORKING

Location: Istanbul, Turkey
Email: nerd@nerdworking.org
Web: www.nerdworking.org

NERDWORKING is a network company which was founded in 2009 to research and develop unique tools for artistic, commercial, experimental interactive media projects catered to public space, fairs and performing arts. Interdisciplinary network comprises and manages artists, illustrators, designers, architects, real-time animation designers, coders, mechatronics, robotics and electronics professionals. The core team's aim is designing new experiences between human, machine and codes.

## Nuno Caroço

Location: Lisbon, Portugal
Tel: +351 916225481
Web: www.nunocaroco.com

Nuno Caroço is an after effects artist with almost 10 years experience working in compositing and post production in Portugal. With a background and M.A in Fine Arts, he has also a passion for painting and analog photography as well as other art areas. Since 1996 he has experienced in pixel manipulation mixing real and digital media. In the past, he professionally created illustrations, interactive animations and motion graphics before he moved into digital compositing. From 2002 to 2009, he worked intensively in the 3D visualization industry, while he worked as Senior Compositor and Technical Director for post production and compositing. Since 2009 he has collaborated with Adobe Portugal. As a partner and influencer, he was invited for the first Adobe Video Community Leader in London in 2010.
His specialties include all types of post production, 2D/3D digital compositing, rotoscoping, matchmoving, color rrading, stereoscopic workflow, VFX shot analysis, pipeline optimization and planning in After Effects and WorkFlow.

## ONIX

Location: La Plata, Buenos Aires, Argentina
Tel: +54 9 221 591 4099
Web: www.onix.ws

ONIX is a motion design studio directed by Leonardo Rica, specialized in visual arts including design and animation. Working with great partners, ONIX is capable of working for worldwide clients covering different areas such as on air TV graphic design, advertising, 2D animation, 3D animation and video postproduction. ONIX has developed many show packs, TV channel IDs, commercial spots, campaign resumes, institutional videos, and so on.

## Onur Senturk

Location: Istanbul, Turkey
Email: hi@onursenturk.tv
Web: onursenturk.tv

Onur Senturk studied traditional painting and figure drawing after completing a traditional animation degree as his B.F.A. He took part in several international and national collaborative exhibitions with works in both prints and time-based media. He designed and animated "Nokta", which won the Honorary Mention award from Prix Ars Electronica in computer animation / film / VFX category. He has been featured in various national and international magazines such as *Stash*, *Computer Arts* and *Motionographer* with interviews, articles and showcases both online and published. He currently works as a freelance designer and director in Istanbul.

## Parasol Island

Address: Neusser Strasse 125, 40219 Düsseldorf, Germany
Tel: +49 211 159220 0
Web: www.parasol-island.com

Parasol Island is a design-loving, round-house kicking production for all forms of digital communication. Aside from the high quality techniques and content that Parasol has exhibited, the clients appreciate their aesthetic standard which has been established throughout recent years, earning Parasol the reputation as a creative source and stronghold for ambitious agencies and sophisticated brands alike. Parasol Island currently employs 40 people. Their biggest gun is the ultra-wide range of services and styles. The Company was founded in 2002 by Charles Bals, Sebastian Druschel, Philip Hansen and Moritz von Schrötter in Düsseldorf and also opened up a space in Berlin.

## Physalia

Address: Pamplona 89, 08018 Barcelona, Spain
Tel: +34 931 822 844
Email: info@physaliastudio.com

Physalia is a motion graphics and visual effects studio in Barcelona. It was established in 2006 and consists of three people: Pablo Barqun, Marcos Coral and Mauro Gimferrer. Since the beginning of foundation, they have carried out research in many fields such as photography, 3D & 2D animation, stop-motion, electronics, mixed media, live action, etc. Their love for electronics impels them to develop tools to shoot things that would be impossible to achieve otherwise. The mix of self-made tools and motion graphics is the inspiration for some of their projects, and when the opportunity arises, they like twisting and pushing the possibilities of the creative process.

## PlusOne

Address: Eerste van Swindenstraat 381, 1093 GB, The Netherlands
Tel: 0031 20 845 18 14
Web: www.plusoneamsterdam.com

PlusOne is an independent Amsterdam-based studio that creates hybrid content in which it combines animation, live action and digital media. Their works are creative extension for advertising agencies, brands and broadcasters who aim at design-infused storytelling with a twist.

## ROAN

Location: Mexico
Email: botecual@hotmail.com
Web: www.be.net/ROAN/frame

ROAN is a 26-year-old graphic designer and illustrator. Born in Mexico City, he studied at the Universidad Autonoma Metropolitan (UAM) and began his career in 2007. He has worked as a full time designer for magazine publishers and various design agencies. In late 2008 he started working for MVS Television, and has mixed it with his work as a freelance illustrator since 2009. In 2010 he was the winner of the PromaxBDA World Gold Rocket Award.

## Rodrigo Miguel

Location: Mexico Distrito Federal, Mexico
Tel: 044 55 18 11 48 88
Web: www.behance.net/rodrigoMiguel; www.weare.com.mx

Rodrigo Miguel aka rO (Mexico, 1982) is a designer and motionographer, graduated from Universidad Autónoma Metropolitana. With an interactive design background, in 2008 rO joined the Once TV Mexico Department of Design. His work has been awarded by Promax / BDA. In 2010, he co-founded the design and animation studio We Are! He is currently developing projects for clients in Mexico and Europe.

## Ryan Brownhill

Loctioon: Texas, USA
Email: ryanbrownhill@gmail.com
Web: www.ryanbrownhill.com

Ryan Brownhill is an undergraduate student currently at the Savannah College of Art and Design, majoring in Motion Media Design. He is originally from Texas. Ryan enjoys experimenting with different mediums, and hopes to exceed in the industry by pushing the boundaries of both himself and the industry.

## Ryunosuke Shimura

Location: Tokyo, Japan
Tel: +81 (0)3 5829 6856
Web: www.maxilla.jp; www.sdthn.com

Born in 1988, Ryunosuke Shimura is enrolled at Tama Art University's Information Art Course currently. Since founding Maxilla inc. in 2009, Shimura has been mainly creating music videos, commercial films and installation works. In 2011, he began developing system applications. Via his company, he works on a wide variety of works that often expands into unconventional media.

## Scott Benson

Location: Pittsburgh, PA, USA
Tel: +814 937 3743
Web: www.bombsfall.com

Scott Benson has been a freelance animator and illustrator since 2005. As a child, he began animating in the margins of old second-hand books. He is a self-taught designer and works primarily in After Effects and Flash. His time is divided between working with clients and creating the independent animated shorts for which he is known. His work has been screened internationally. Apart from animation, Scott spends his time drawing and making homemade prints. He lives in Pittsburgh with his wife and his cat.

## Scott Pagano

Location: Los Angeles, CA, USA
Tel: +1 310 397 9890
Web: www.neither-field.com

Scott Pagano is a hybrid fine artist and independent creative professional recognized for his high-end, multi-media works. Simultaneously cinematic, photographic and synthetic, Pagano's visual works offer a window into the future of new media art. Pagano works independently and with globally recognized production companies to produce engaging moving images for a wide range of projects including cinema, broadcast, online, and experiential. Neither-Field functions as production umbrella for his various projects and endeavors.

## Selfburning

Adress: Flat 136, Kulikovskaya Street 7, Moscow, Russia.
Tel: +7 (926) 304 35 57; + 7 (916)331 79 59
Web: www.selfburning.com

Selfburning is an independent and non-commercial project organized by two people. They started doing short experimental video and animation in 2006. Now actively collaborating with artists, photographers and musicians.

## Serge Tardif

Location: Montreal, Quebec, Canada
Email: info@sergetardif.com
Web: www.sergetardif.com

As a freelance graphic, web and motion designer, Serge Tardif lives in Montreal. He has worked as a photographer, artist and graphic designer for more than 15 years since he studies painting in Ottawa University, Ontario, Canada. Serge Tardif has invested his time in lots of projects including theater set, advertising illustration, web design and motion graphic.

## Sergey Rybkin

Location: Moscow, Russia
Email: s_e_r@mail.ru
Web: www.behance.net/dabezi

Sergey Rybkin is a motion designer in Moscow. He stepped in the field of motion design in 2007, which marks the beginning of his career. Sergey Rybkin has worked for various channels. Now he is working for MTV-Russia.

## Shah Azman

Location: Selangor Darul Ehsan, Malaysia
Tel: +60123705114
Web: www.behance.net/shahazman; pf37.tumblr.com

Shah Azman is a self-expressive young visual artist. He's known for his passion in various arts and design disciplines: illustrations, doodles, motion designs, masks, costume making and other forms of visual arts. Graduated from Film & Animation at the Multimedia University, Malaysia, he is influenced by superheroes and his childhood imaginations – to save the world, to be free. He's won Astro's NCA Awards 2009 under the category of Outstanding Music Video, and has been featured in a few local art magazines. Now he is a motion designer and art director at Motiofixo.

## Somatic AV

Location: Berlin, Germany
Tel: +49 0157 765 718 33
Web: www.somaticav.com; www.behance.net/Solanina/frame

Somatic AV is a design studio developed by Giovanni Conti and Sara Meloni. They focus on the design of interactive environments based on realtime synthesis and sequencing of audiovisual contents that react to the energies enlivening the installation space, generating continuously changing organic realistic landscapes. They use these environments as playful spaces or as counterparts to balance the specific issues suggested by the perceptual analysis of the installation site.

## Studio Mica

Location: Istanbul, Turkey
Tel: +90 212 245 0114
Web: www.studiomica.com

Mica is an animation studio focusing on creative productions for advertising, motion graphics, and TV series. Founded in 2010 by Luca Schenato and Sinem Vardarlı Schenato, two animation directors with the past of 3D supervisors, art directors & animators. Studio Mica designs, directs and creates animations in a varied range of styles and techniques with an innovative approach. The studio offers a complete production for animation filmmaking and works from the first steps of the film, like concept, character design, screenplay, art direction to the final creations.

## Sulfurica

Address: Roman Díaz 1271, Providencia, Santiago, Chile
Tel: +56 2 440 82 09
Web: www.portafolio.sulfurica.tv

Sulfurica Motion Design Studio is located in Santiago de Chile and is made up of talented young professionals. They specialize and provide art direction, 3D animation, music videos, artwork, visual branding, films and advertisement, getting involved in any step of the creative process, from the beginning of the conceptualization, through the development of storyboards, to the final product.

## Takafumi Tsuchiya

Location: Tokyo, Japan
Email: imagesandtechnology@gmail.com
Web: www.takafumitsuchiya.com

Takafumi Tsuchiya is a Tokyo-based independent motion director, designer and animator. In 2002, he was graduated from the art department of Nihon University with the specialty of cinema. He has created some video art works and worked as a video jockey. His works were created for both commercial and artistic purposes without any boundaries. He has collaborated and performed live with a lot of cutting-edge musicians, not only at cultural events but night parties.

## The Fridge

Location: Brussels, Belgium
Email: tom@thefridge.tv
Web: www.thefridge.tv

As a post production facility located in Brussels, Belgium The Fridge was founded in 2004 by Jan Hameeuw. The team has worked on several feature films and music videos over the years. The Fridge has built up a strong reputation in the Belgian VFX world.

## The Neighbourhood

Location: Manchester, England
Tel: +01612449500
Web: www.the-neighbourhood.com

The Neighborhood is a design studio located in England.They work with clients in advertising, design, broadcast, architecture and beyond. The Neighborhood has designed for Sony Playstation, Sony Europe, Land Securities, AHMM, Manchester Airport, BBC, CBBC and many other famous clients.

## Tridente Brand Firm

Location: Monterrey, Mexico
Tel: +52 81 83352646
Web: www.tridente.mx

Tridente Brand Firm is a branding-centered agency with multidisciplinary skills. Covering from graphic design to advanced HD video production, through campaign strategies. Awarded in the 5 Seconds Project by Greyscale Gorilla, VisualOrgasm, Linkage, FaveUp, Designaside, GOUW and MOWSNET.

## UPPER FIRST

Location: Malmoe. Sweden
Tel: +46 706 979 293
Web: www.upperfirst.com

UPPER FIRST is a studio aimed at producing visual FX, motion graphics and film for the growing digital and new media market. There are six founding members sharing a mutual interest in design, direction and visual production. Built on a foundation of creativity, credibility and freedom of thought, their productions entice the imagination beyond the expected. Through the value of awe and entertainment their communication aims are to increase brand value and awareness.

## UrbanGeek aka Michael Fawke

Location: Cornwall, England
Tel: +00 44 7796 141110
Web: www.michaelfawke.co.uk; www.urbangeek.org

UrbanGeek aka Michael Fawke is a 25-year-old motion designer and 3D artist. Currently he is a student of graphic design completing his final year of study at University College Falmouth. Michael has a genuine passion for creativity, inspired by culture, architecture, photography, visual communication, typography, fashion and fine art. With a passion for digital, Michael has specialized in interactive and 3D moving image; his approach makes use of a diverse range of skills, techniques and software. During his time at University Michael has covered a wide variety of projects through interactive installations, branding, packaging, and design for print, web, advertising, photography and videographer for both personal and live commercial projects.

## YanTing Chen

Location: New York, NY
Email: tony14752000@gmail.com
Web: www.yantingchen.com

YanTing Chen is an international award-winning designer based in New York and Taiwan. He specializes in graphic design, motion graphics and web design. He earned his BFA in Communication Design from National Taiwan University of Science and Technology in 2007. YanTing has won more than 80 international design awards. In 2009, he was selected by *La Vie Magazine* as one of Taiwan's top 100 designers and was profiled in their recently published bestseller: *Top 100 Designers of Taiwan*. YanTing's works have been exhibited all over the world, from New York to Germany, Taiwan, Los Angeles, China and Bolivia.

## Zapum

Location: Lisbon, Portugal
Email: zapum@hotmail.com
Web: www.zapum.org; www.nunojpereira.com

Zapum Aka Nuno Pereira is a designer based in Lisbon, Portugal. Besides motion design, he also creates graphic works as a freelance designer. He likes creating stories and challenges himself to learn something new in every project by involving himself in new fields to learn different techniques, which is always for fun!

**MOVING GRAPHICS:**
New directions in motion design
Les nouvelles tendances du motion design
Nuevas tendencias en animación gráfica
Nuove direzioni nel design in movimento

COPYRIGHT © 2012 DOPRESS BOOKS (www.dopress.com)
COPYRIGHT © 2012 English language edition published by
Promopress for sale worldwide except Asia.

Translators of the foreword: English (revision) / French / Spanish / Italian: Satèl.lit bcn - Hugo Steckelmacher / Sylvie Mathis /
Miguel Izquierdo / Arrigo Frisano-Paulon
Cover Design: Stan van Steendam
Layout Copyright: Dopress Books
Editing Team: Dopress Books

PROMOPRESS is a commercial brand of:
Promotora de Prensa Internacional S.A.
C/ Ausiàs March 124
08013 Barcelona, Spain
Phone: +34 93 245 14 64
Fax:     +34 93 265 48 83
info@promopress.es
www.promopress.es
www.promopresseditions.com

ISBN: 978-84-92810-46-8

Printed in China.